Plays By
Jeremy Dobrish

Broadway Play Publishing Inc

New York

BroadwayPlayPub.com

Plays By Jeremy Dobrish

First printing: June 1999
I S B N: 978-0-88145-157-3

Book design: Marie Donovan
Copy editing: Liam Brosnahan
Typeface: Palatino

CONTENTS

ABOUT THE AUTHOR

Jeremy Dobrish is the Artistic Director of the adobe theatre company which he co-founded in 1991. adobe's unique style has enabled it to become one of New York's most celebrated theater groups. Jeremy's plays for adobe include the critically acclaimed NOTIONS IN MOTION, which moved Off-Broadway; THE HANDLESS MAIDEN, which he recently adapted for the screen; and BLINK OF AN EYE. His directing credits for adobe include DUET! with Erin Quinn Purcell and Gregory Jackson; LARRY AND THE WEREWOLF and THE EIGHT, both by Jeff Goode; as well as his own plays NOTIONS IN MOTION and BLINK OF AN EYE. Jeremy also directs the comedy team Slovin and Allen.

Jeremy is a member of The Dramatists Guild and has spoken at N Y U, Wesleyan, Brown, and Hofstra, and served on panels for The Dramatists Guild and The Drama League on the topic of producing and directing your own work.

ACKNOWLEDGMENTS

I'd like to thank Kip Gould at Broadway Play Publishing and Peter Hagan at Gersh for having an early belief that what I had to say was something other people might like to hear. Thanks also to my family, particularly my father, for always believing in me. Thanks to Beth for giving me so much inspiration and support.

And a major thank you to everyone at adobe. These plays were not created in a vacuum. They were developed through the constant input of a group of highly skilled and intelligent theater artists. Without their help, I never would have started or continued to write. Finally, thank you to Christopher Roberts, who always believed we were destined to do great things.

A quick note about the plays: These plays are meant to be performed.
They are canvases upon which a director must take a strong stand.
They are words that leave many empty spaces for the actors to fill in. They need to be big. They need to be fun. You need to get inside them and make them yours. They need to move, fluid and fast. They are plays that require imagination and ambition. But if you trust them, they will reward you.

BLINK OF AN EYE

ORIGINAL PRODUCTION

BLINK OF AN EYE was first presented by the adobe theatre company, opening on 15 September 1995. The cast and creative contributors were:

MASON/GUARD ONE/SOOTHSAYER	Jay Rosenbloom
DRAKE/GUARD TWO	Joe West
BOSWELL TWO/JULIUS CAESAR	Henry Caplan
DIRECTOR/MR FARQUAR/BRUTUS	Matthew Aibel
BOSWELL	Arthur Aulisi
JOE/ANNOUNCER/CLERK	Christopher Marobella
PAUL FARQUAR	Vin Knight
KIKI FARQUAR/ABACAB	Kathryn Langwell
MATTHEW FARQUAR	Arthur Halpern
CELESTE/SIMONE	Erin Quinn Purcell

Director	Jeremy Dobrish
Sets	Steven Capone
Lighting	Paul Ziemer
Costumes	Meganne George
Sound	Chris Todd
Dramaturg	Sonya Sobieski

CHARACTERS

Mason/Guard One/Soothsayer
Drake/Guard Two
Boswell Two/Julius Caesar
Director/Mr Farquar/Brutus
Boswell
Joe/Announcer/Clerk
Paul Farquar
Kiki Farquar/Abacab
Matthew Farquar
Celeste/Simone

(As the lights come up, the actors playing MASON, DRAKE, *and* BOSWELL TWO *begin to take their places. Suddenly everyone freezes and* CELESTE *enters.* CELESTE *is an angel dressed in white.)*

CELESTE: "Blink of an Eye." A three-act play meant to be performed in three seconds. In all likelihood, we're going to take a little bit longer tonight. *(Gives the date)* "Blink of an Eye." Act one. Second one.

(Slide: "Tracker". The lights reveal MASON *and* DRAKE, *two thugs, on a dock.)*

MASON: You think Boswell can find this guy?

DRAKE: You kidding me? He's the best.

*(*BOSWELL TWO *on a "boat" "paddles" his way over to* MASON *and* DRAKE *on the dock.)*

MASON: Well, well, well. The man of the hour.

BOSWELL TWO: Mason. Drake.

MASON: So, where is he?

BOSWELL TWO: I haven't found him. Yet. My guess is he's trying to outrun himself.

MASON: But you're sure he's alive.

BOSWELL TWO: Oh I'm sure.

DRAKE: We gotta find him.

BOSWELL TWO: "Oh, I'll find him. He's alive I'll find him".

(The DIRECTOR *enters from the audience with* BOSWELL.*)*

DIRECTOR: O.K. Great. I like that thing you're doing with your fingers. That definitely works. Let's keep that. What did you think?

BOSWELL: I don't know. He's good.

DIRECTOR: He is good, isn't he? A play about a Tracker who can find anyone. It can't miss.

BOSWELL: I like the two other guys too. They make scary bad guys. Wrong costumes, though.

DIRECTOR: You don't like the costumes?

BOSWELL: Real ones don't dress like that.

DIRECTOR: Real bad guys?

BOSWELL: That's right.

DIRECTOR: O K, we'll work on the costumes. Why don't you guys take ten.

(MASON *and* DRAKE *exit.*)

BOSWELL TWO: O K if I split?

DIRECTOR: Sure, we're back tomorrow at nine.

BOSWELL TWO: No sweat. It's an honor to meet you by the way.

BOSWELL: Oh...uh, thanks.

(BOSWELL TWO *exits.*)

DIRECTOR: Fabulous actor.

BOSWELL: Where's he off to?

DIRECTOR: He's in another show at the moment. Julius Caesar. He's brilliant. You should see it if you can. Anyway...other than the costumes...

BOSWELL: Other than the costumes, it's good.

DIRECTOR: Good? Good? That's it? Boswell, this play's gonna immortalize you. You could die tomorrow, it wouldn't matter. You'll be remembered forever.

BOSWELL: I know, it's just that...

DIRECTOR: What?

BOSWELL: Well...I can't really find everyone.

DIRECTOR: Who can't you find?

BOSWELL: What?

DIRECTOR: Tell me.

BOSWELL: No one.

DIRECTOR: Exactly.

BOSWELL: I don't want to talk about it.

DIRECTOR: Boswell, it's a play.

BOSWELL: Yeah, I know, but I mean it makes me out like I'm some kind of a comic book superhero.

DIRECTOR: It's dramatic license. You can't be so hung up on reality. Who cares what you really did, who you truly are? This is theatre. This is illusion.

BOSWELL: I just think you should make it clear that I can't really find everyone. I'm just a regular bounty hunter.

DIRECTOR: It all becomes clear at the end. Don't worry about a thing. Trust me.

BOSWELL: I trust you.

DIRECTOR: That's what I like to hear. You need a ride uptown?

BOSWELL: Nah, I'm gonna get a cab, grab a quick bite, and call it a day.

DIRECTOR: Alright. And hey, Boswell, remember, I care about *you*.

(BOSWELL *and the* DIRECTOR *exit.* JOE *is revealed in the diner.*)

JOE: It began with a sound: a ring. It rang three times. Once for each second. Loud and violent. The kind of ringing that resonates inside you and rattles your brain. The kind of ring you never expect. The kind that signals bad news and sets in motion events that can never be undone. How do you make sense of a ring like that? How do you change your consciousness to allow the existence of such a ring into your world?

(BOSWELL *enters the diner. Suspended above the counter is a T V showing a Knicks game as well as a clock showing ten o'clock. Slide:"Next Thing You Know...")*

BOSWELL: Hey, Joe. Gimme a coffee, will ya?

JOE: Comin up, Bos. (*Referring to the T V*) Oh, for Christ's sake. Ridiculous game. Refs won't cut Ewing any slack. Keeps getting called for "three seconds".

BOSWELL: Tough break. I usually like to stay home when the Knicks play. Watch the game. Sometimes I don't even pay attention to what's going on, I just like to watch.

JOE: Yup.

BOSWELL: Had to be at the theater tonight, though.

JOE: Yeah?

BOSWELL: New play they're doing called "Tracker". Based loosely on my experiences, you know?

JOE: You're shittin' me. Congratulations.

BOSWELL: Yeah. Thanks. They're doing a good job. I just wish they'd be a little more faithful to who I truly am.

JOE: Pfff.

BOSWELL: What?

JOE: Who among us knows who he truly is? (*Pause*)

BOSWELL: How's Alice?

JOE: She's fine..., thanks.

BOSWELL: Glad to hear it.

JOE: Hey, it's supposed to snow tonight, you hear that?

BOSWELL: Snow? It's the middle of September.

JOE: Greenhouse effect. No ozone. World's coming to an end. Earthquake'll hit California, half the state'll fall into the ocean. Whole world's crumbling. What can you do?

BOSWELL: Nothing, I guess.

JOE: There's a law of diminishing returns or something on disaster, though.

(BOSWELL *notices something, maybe a pinspot, crawling on the counter like a cockroach.*)

BOSWELL: What's that?

JOE: You know, like as far as feeling tragedy is concerned. It's like for us five million dead in China equals five thousand dead in California equals fifty dead in New York equals someone killed your brother.

(*The pinspot is becoming all-absorbing of* BOSWELL's *attention.*)

BOSWELL: What?

JOE: Any of which could happen at any time.

BOSWELL: Uh-huh.

JOE: The whole world's turning to shit in the blink of an eye. It's unbelievable. Anything can get you. One second you're just sitting there, next thing you know.... (*He snaps his fingers.*)

(BOSWELL *slams his fist on the pinspot. The payphone rings. Loud. In a separate area the lights reveal* MATTHEW FARQUAR *swinging a lead pipe. The phone rings a second time. Loud. The lights reveal in a separate area* BRUTUS *with a knife raised above his head. The phone rings a third time. Loud. The lights reveal in a separate area* SIMONE *the angel who holds out a cup of tea as an offering.* SIMONE *is dressed in black. The lights return to the diner. The Knicks game is frozen on the T V.* JOE *answers the phone.*)

JOE: Joe's. You are, are you? Let me see if he's here, hang on a second. Hey, Bos, you expecting a call?

BOSWELL: No.

JOE: Sorry, I don't think he's here right now. Oh it is, huh? Hang on. Guy says it's important.

BOSWELL: Hello? Yes, it is. Yeah, I can find people. Uh-huh. Alright. Sure, we can meet. Where? Nice address. I'll see you there tomorrow at nine.

JOE: Everything alright?

BOSWELL: Yeah, sure. Guy named Paul Farquar.

(*We hear an ominous chord from an organ.*)

JOE: Paul Farquar? Not billionaire eccentric muckity-muck Paul Farquar?

BOSWELL: Who's that?

JOE: Paul Farquar? Guy's richer than Trump. He owns everything.

BOSWELL: Never heard of him.

JOE: They say he's made of magic.

BOSWELL: He says he needs me to find his brother.

JOE: Wow. Paul Farquar has a missing brother.

BOSWELL: I guess. *(He taps his watch and holds it to his ear.)* Well, I'm outa here, Joe. Time to hit the hay. Say a prayer for the Knicks.

JOE: Take it easy, Bos.

(Blackout. The sound of a grandfather clock striking ten a little too quickly. Slide:"Triple Touch". Lights up on PAUL FARQUAR and KIKI. They address the audience as though it were BOSWELL.)

PAUL: Hello, Mr Boswell. I'm Paul Farquar.

KIKI: I'm Kiki.

PAUL: I can't tell you how much I appreciate you coming to see me.

KIKI: Kiki Farquar.

PAUL: Mr Boswell, I'm going to tell you some things you might find hard to believe.

KIKI: I'm Paul's wife.

PAUL: But I need you to take me seriously, and so I'm going to show you something.

KIKI: It's basically a trick.

PAUL: It's not a trick, it's a power.

KIKI: Excuse me, it's a power.

PAUL: That's right. Now then, do you remember that man from that television program a decade or two back?

KIKI: "Soap". Why don't you just say "Soap"? I'm sure he knows the show.

PAUL: Soap. The man on Soap who would snap his fingers twice quickly in succession and believed that in so doing he could render himself completely invisible?

KIKI: Richard Mulligan's character. Oh..., what was his name? Why don't you just say "Richard Mulligan's character"?

PAUL: Richard Mulligan's character. Well, I can do that. For real. I'm sure the notion intrigues you. Wouldn't you like to be able to snap your fingers twice quickly in succession and in so doing render yourself completely invisible?

KIKI: It's quite a trick. You're gonna love it.

PAUL: It's not a trick. There is much you can learn from television, Mr Boswell. The snaps of Mulligan. The blinks of Jeannie. The nose twitch of Samantha.

KIKI: Get to the snapping.

PAUL: I'm getting to it. I am afraid to do it for you, Mr Boswell, because I know it would frighten you. What would it mean if you were actually sitting across from a man with such powers? It would shatter your conception of reality and what is possible and why.

KIKI: You're so over-dramatic. Just snap your fingers already and get to the story.

PAUL: Will you shut up? I'm sorry, Mr Boswell...but I must find a way to make you believe my fantastical story, and so I must prove to you that I am for real. Alright, I'll do it for you.

(He looks about as if to make sure no one is watching. He snaps his fingers like Richard Mulligan on "Soap" and all the lights go out. After a moment we hear two quick snaps and the lights are restored. KIKI applauds and hoots.)

PAUL: I did it. I snapped my fingers twice quickly in succession and in so doing I rendered myself completely invisible.

KIKI: Not bad, huh?

PAUL: Perhaps you are skeptical. Maybe you think the lights simply went out for a moment. The lights in the room between you and me that allow us to see each other. Or perhaps it was these stage lights here which allow the audience to see us. Perhaps those were the lights that went out. Or maybe, just maybe, when I snapped my fingers, we all, every single one of us in the world blinked at the same time and entire worlds crumbled and reassembled themselves in the time it took our collective unconscious to close and reopen our eyes.

KIKI: It doesn't matter.

PAUL: What matters is that it happened when I snapped my fingers twice quickly in succession. If you snapped your fingers twice quickly in succession nothing at all would happen. You should therefore listen very carefully to what I have to tell you. Lives depend on it.

KIKI: Oh my God! How rude we are. I'm so sorry, Mr Boswell, we didn't offer you any tea. I hope you'll forgive our manners.

(KIKI picks up a servant's bell and shakes it violently over her head. It has no clapper, but the sound comes over the speakers. On the first ring the lights reveal in

a separate area the two GUARDS *who look around themselves, confused.* KIKI *shakes the bell again, and the lights reveal in a separate area* CELESTE *the angel shaking her head "no."* KIKI *shakes a third time, and the lights reveal in a separate area* JULIUS CAESAR *with a knife in his heart. His face shows pain and surprise. The lights return to* KIKI *and* PAUL, *who plays nervously with his ring. Sand begins to fall down the wall throughout the rest of the scene.)*

KIKI: So get to the story already.

PAUL: Turning myself invisible is nothing compared to what I am about to tell you. I am one of three brothers, Mr Boswell. Identical triplets. And I am inexplicably linked to them. More than what the outside world might consider normal.

KIKI: That's for sure.

PAUL: I have what I call triple touch. When you touch an object it is single touch, you feel it in one place. When you touch yourself it is double touch, you feel it in two places. It's what teaches you the limits of your physical existence. Well, sometimes...sometimes, I have triple touch with my brothers. I feel what they feel and vice versa. Prick one of them and I will bleed with him.

(We hear the sound of a faraway scream.)

KIKI: It's unbelievably annoying.

PAUL: My brother Matthew is the worst of us. He simply cannot distinguish between himself and "other". Can you imagine, Mr Boswell, not being able to distinguish where you end and someone else begins? Feeling things that aren't happening to you?

(We hear the sound of a faraway scream.)

KIKI: Happens at the most inopportune moments.

PAUL: At an early age I was separated from my brothers for reasons I don't wish to go into.

KIKI: You can tell him why.

PAUL: I don't think I should, dear.

KIKI: Why not? Go ahead and tell him.

PAUL: Are you going to let me do this? We agreed that you were going to let me do this.

KIKI: Fine.

PAUL: I'm sorry, Mr Boswell.

KIKI: I just think you should tell him about your father, and about the gangsters, and about how you and your brothers got separated. I think it might help him.

PAUL: Fine, you tell him.

KIKI: I'm not gonna tell him.

PAUL: Good. Then can I get on with the story?

KIKI: I wish you would.

PAUL: Thank you.

KIKI: Who's stopping you?

PAUL: Where was I?

KIKI: You were separated from your brothers.

PAUL: Yes, and one of my brothers, Matthew, went quite insane from the separation. Because his madness was so violent he ended up in the state penitentiary.

KIKI: To say that Matthew is "a very unpleasant person" would be an awfully kind way of putting things.

PAUL: My other brother, James, somehow managed to handle the separation the best. Like Matthew he was originally sent to live in a foster home. I have no idea what became of him. No one does, and despite my best attempts, I simply cannot find him.

KIKI: Poor bastard.

PAUL: Matthew was much easier to find. I, of course, am the third and final brother. I grew up with my uncle and, as you can see, I have managed to do quite well for myself.

KIKI: Alright, no need to show off.

PAUL: Matthew, my incarcerated and insane brother, is under the mistaken impression that James and I are autonomous embodiments of himself.

KIKI: In other words, he believes that there are literally three of him walking around. Or at least three living sides of him.

PAUL: That's right. And as you can imagine, Mr Boswell, that is not a comforting thought. There cannot be more than one of you and so my brother Matthew, whom I visit from time to time, has warned me that he will escape from his prison cell tomorrow. He will hunt down his brothers and kill us without mercy.

KIKI: Oh my god. I can't even hear this.

PAUL: Because of my money, I will be harder to murder. No one knows what happened to James, so he will be more difficult to find but easier to kill. What Matthew doesn't understand is the triple touch. If he succeeds in killing James, the three of us will all die at once.

KIKI: Oh, Paul.

PAUL: As you can imagine, Mr Boswell, that is not an option I particularly care for. You are my final hope.

KIKI: Please help us.

PAUL: I need you to find James and tell him who he is and that he is in danger. In saving James, you will save me, and for these services I am prepared to pay you quite handsomely.

KIKI: That is an understatement, believe me.

PAUL: I implore you to save me by finding James.

(SIMONE *enters as a servant, carrying a tray on which are three cups of tea.*)

KIKI: How many lumps, Mr Boswell?

(*Blackout. The sound of a grandfather clock striking ten a little too quickly. Lights up on the clock. It ticks one second forward. Lights up on* BOSWELL'S *apartment where* BOSWELL *enters and flips on the T V. Slide: "Your True Self". The* ANNOUNCER *steps out of the shadows. A hollow television set frames his head.*)

ANNOUNCER: ...and the amazing thing is—it's not expensive. It's a major purchase, yes. It'll play a role in your life unlike any other, but for a limited time only, we're practically giving it away. And best of all, death comes with a thirty-day money-back guarantee. But, believe me, you are going to love this little baby. I know it seems strange. You might be thinking, "Death? But I'm afraid of death. I'm not so sure I want a little death right about now." Well, let's go to our first testimonial. You know him, you love him. Star of stage, screen, and of course...history, let's have a nice warm welcome for Mr Julius Caesar.

(JULIUS CAESAR *enters to the sound of applause.*)

CAESAR: Cowards die many times before their death;
The valiant never taste of death but once.
Of all the wonders that I have yet heard,
It seems to me most strange that men should fear,
Seeing that death, a necessary end,
Will come when it come.

ANNOUNCER: Alright..., Mr Julius Caesar, everyone.

(*The sound of applause as* CAESAR *exits.*)

ANNOUNCER: Now, see, he was apprehensive at first. But eventually he came around. He took death home to see how he liked it and became one of our most satisfied customers. Now, I know you've heard the hype. The floating above your body, seeing the tunnel, seeing the light, hearing the voice. Well, new and improved death will take you one step further. All the way home to your own personalized demise, where you will discover your true self. You and your true self will spend eternity together, and you will learn who you really are and what your destiny was. It's a beautiful feeling, folks. No hell. No worms nibbling away at your body. There are so many misconceptions out there that give our product a bad name. Death can be fun.

(SIMONE *enters, does tricks, tries to entertain, etc.*)

ANNOUNCER: Does death look like this?

(*A slide of the grim reaper. The sound of the "studio audience" saying "no"*)

ANNOUNCER: Does death look like this? (*A slide of the devil. The sound of the studio audience saying "no"*) Does death look like this?

(*A slide of* BOSWELL'*s face. The sound of the studio audience saying "maybe"*)

ANNOUNCER: Very good. Now, remember, death comes with a full lifetime warranty. No, that's a joke. But if you call today we will send you the complete death instructional home video as well as an autographed copy of "Standing Tall: The Rise and Rise of Patrick Ewing". And remember, folks, death is not sold in any stores, so do yourself a favor, and call today.

(*The lights fade out on the* ANNOUNCER *and up on* KIKI.)

KIKI: That night Boswell had a dream. He dreamt that he was in love with a woman named Kiki and that his name was Elton. In the dream he was glad to be free of the name Boswell. He dreamt that he and Kiki had their own television show together, which ended every week with her declaring that she was quite a little bit country and he insisting that, despite all the hijinks they had gotten into that week, he remained just a little bit rock and roll.

(*The lights crossfade to two prison guards. In a separate area, restrained by shackles, is* MATTHEW FARQUAR.)

GUARD ONE: So you're the new guy?

GUARD TWO: Yup. Anything I need to know?

GUARD ONE: Need to know?

GUARD TWO: Yeah, you know, like is there anything especially dangerous about this one?

GUARD ONE: Look, pal, I don't know what you're used to, but this is a maximium security prison. And this is the cell that puts the "maximium" in "maximum security." If he's in here...he's a little dangerous.

GUARD TWO: Hey, no need to be a dick about it. I'm just asking if there's anything special I should know.

GUARD ONE: They didn't brief you on this guy?

(GUARD TWO *shrugs.*)

GUARD ONE: This guy is haunted. I mean really fucking haunted. I mean all the crazies talk to themselves and yell at nobody and shit like that, but this guy is really possessed.

GUARD TWO: Possessed? Like how?

GUARD ONE: Well...sometimes he starts bleeding. Just out of nowhere, starts bleeding. One time he developed an actual gunshot wound. No gun, no bullet, but this guy's got a real, doctor-certified, gunshot wound.

GUARD TWO: Really?

GUARD ONE: Yeh-heh. Sometimes, the bastard doesn't even pee. For days, I'm talking about, weeks even. Just goes without peeing. It's like someone else is peeing for him. I never seen anything like it.

GUARD TWO: He ever give you any trouble? I mean...personally?

GUARD ONE: Me? Nah. He likes me. Besides, that's the great thing about guarding the real loons: It's actualy the easiest job you could ask for. These fruitloops are so well restrained and doped up, there's no way they're gonna try anything.

GUARD TWO: You never had one escape on you?

GUARD ONE: Escape? What, are you out of your mind? You can't escape out of a place like this.

(MATTHEW *snaps his fingers twice and the shackles fly away. He walks right in front of the guards.*)

GUARD TWO: I had a guy escape on me once. Back when I was out west.

GUARD ONE: Yeah? You shoot him?

GUARD TWO: No, you kidding? Never even saw him. Shit, you don't break out of jail by walking past the guards. You break out of jail by swimming through miles of sewer shit, emptying your sorry ass into the river, and swimming to freedom.

GUARD ONE: Amen to that.

(*A spotlight hits* MATTHEW. *He smiles and walks casually offstage. An alarm goes off.*)

GUARD TWO: HOLY SHIT! IT'S HAPPENING AGAIN! AAHHHRGGH! ESCAPE? HELP ME! MOMMY!

GUARD ONE: Will you relax? Hey! Hey! (*He slaps* GUARD TWO.) It's a false alarm I'm sure.

GUARD TWO: What?

GUARD ONE: I don't know about the pansy-ass place where you used to work, but I'm telling you, it's impossible to break out of this joint.

(Blackout. Slide: "The Piss In Your Soup". MATTHEW *arrives at Port Authority. We hear the sounds of buses, people, etc.)*

MATTHEW: I am Matthew Farquar and I am loony-tunes. A bad-mama-jama. Stay out of my way, oh boy, or I will do something only a crazy man would do. Because I have nothing to lose. I am dark, evil, and sick. I'm the shadow that follows you, the bump in the night, and the monster under your bed. I'm the dissected frog in your locker, the car wreck you strain your neck to see, and the pimple on the end of your nose. I am the piss in your soup, the pebble in your shoe, and the addiction that haunts you late at night. I'm your thumb slammed in a door, a kick in the stomach, and the pus in your wound. I am the headache that will not go away. *(He stops a moment to bite something off his thumbnail.)* I'm a missed free-throw, a sacked quarterback, and strike three in the bottom of the ninth. I'm a bad marriage, a clubbed seal, and the nerve ending at the root of your tooth. I am nails scratching across the blackboard, baby, ha-ha-ha. I am hell on earth, a living nightmare, and the sweat on your sheets. I am fear, loathing, and hatred. I'm the bully after school, lard ass! I am sickness, rot, and decay. I'm a premature ejaculation, a faked orgasm, and your lover's deceitful secret. I am white noise, black rain, and dead skin. *(Pause)* So...anyone want to get a drink with me after the show?

(Blackout. The lights reveal BOSWELL *following* MATTHEW *as he walks a pattern across the stage. They are flanked by the two* GUARDS. *Slide:"Et Tu, Brute?")*

GUARD TWO: Luckily, Boswell had found plenty of escaped convicts in his day. So he did a little guesswork and finding Matthew at Port Authority turned out to be easier than he thought. As soon as he saw his mark, he knew he had succeeded. He was simply stunned by how much Matthew looked like Paul. Absolutely identical twins. They could have literally been the same man.

GUARD ONE: So he followed his mark as discreetly as he could, trying to fall into the other's rhythms, expecting him to seek out James, right? Figuring that Matthew would lead him right to his destination. But he didn't.

*(*MATTHEW *and* BOSWELL *sit in the audience as* JULIUS CAESAR *and* BRUTUS *take the stage in traditional Roman costumes.)*

GUARD TWO: Turns out they ended up going to the theatre to see this really long and boring production of *Julius Caesar.* But until they actually got to the theatre Boswell had no idea that's where he was headed.

GUARD ONE: He didn't even know there were theaters in Soho. He had to sit on these stackable chairs, and for some strange reason the theater was named after some jerkwater state in the Midwest. *(N B: Please feel free to insert your own inside reference to your particular theater.)*

*(*CAESAR *gets stabbed.)*

GUARD TWO: Caesar's death seemed to take forever, and as he was being stabbed, the actor appeared to break out of his character.

CAESAR: (Breaking character) Sweet Thunderin' Jesus that hurts! A KNIFE TO THE HEART!? Bloody friggin' hell that's nasty! OH FUCK ME THAT KNIFE'S A BITCH!

GUARD TWO: Finally Caesar said the line...:

CAESAR: (Back in character) Et tu, Brute? Then fall Caesar. (He dies.)

GUARD TWO: When the play was over, the mark jumped up to his feet and applauded...all by himself.

(The actors leave the stage.)

GUARD ONE: Then Matthew headed up to St Mark's place and entered a real dive of a hotel.

(MATTHEW exits.)

GUARD ONE: Boswell followed him and thought he should wait a bit, you know? Just to make sure his mark had definitely settled in for the night. So he went to a stoop across the street and sat down.

(ABACAB drives her cab past BOSWELL.)

ABACAB: (She gives the date.) "Blink Of An Eye" Act Two. Second Two.

GUARD TWO: He was spent from all of the walking around. He rubbed his tired eyes and when he opened them it seemed as though time had literally stopped. All of the people walking in the street were completely frozen in mid-stride. The water from a taxicab-splashed puddle remained at the height of its arc, headed straight for Boswell's feet. The world was completely silent.

(Slide: "The Eternity Of An Instant". Lights up on BOSWELL sitting on a stoop. CELESTE enters with some McDonald's french fries and sits next to BOSWELL.)

CELESTE: Fry?

BOSWELL: What's going on?

CELESTE: I'm offering you a fry. They're goooood.

BOSWELL: Why is everything frozen?

CELESTE: I stopped time.

BOSWELL: Stopped time?

CELESTE: You know, people have the strangest ideas about time. Like eternity, for instance. Eternity is not time continuing on forever, stretched out infinitely. Eternity is simply the standing still of an instant.

BOSWELL: Who are you exactly?

CELESTE: Oh, I'm sorry. I'm Celeste. I'm your Guardian Angel. I know you so well, sometimes I forget you don't know me.

BOSWELL: You're my Guardian Angel?

CELESTE: Mmm-hmm. You sure you don't want a fry?

BOSWELL: Yes, I'm sure, thank you. Why is my Guardian Angel here?

CELESTE: Please, call me Celeste.

BOSWELL: Alright. Why are you here, Celeste?

CELESTE: Well...I want you to forgive me.

BOSWELL: You want me to...forgive you for what?

CELESTE: Well, you see, being a Guardian Angel is not the greatest job you could ever ask for. I mean, yes, you get certain perks. Stopping time's not bad, free fries, whatever, but basically it's a pretty low self-esteem kind of a deal. No matter how hard you try, you're destined to fail, right? I mean I can watch and watch and watch and be your guardian and help out as best I can. But, ultimately, one of these days (and I'm not saying it's coming anytime soon O K? So don't get all freaky and weird on me) but one of these days someone or something's gonna act too quickly for me to react and you're gonna get yours.

BOSWELL: I am?

CELESTE: I mean, it's not like you're my only client, you know what I'm saying? I've got a lot of people to look out for. Not to mention the animals, although I must admit the cats are a little easier, 'cause at least I can blow it a few times with them so I don't really watch my cats too closely. Oh, but don't get me wrong...I like cats. People...they try to be in the past, present, and future all at the same time, while cats live only in the present, in the eternity of an instant. Ever notice that?

BOSWELL: I don't think that I have.

CELESTE: Well, it's true. But I'm getting away from the point.

BOSWELL: You're saying that you want me to forgive you because ultimately I'm going to die?

CELESTE: Yes. That's exactly it. Couldn't have said it better myself. I've always liked your succinct qualities. Would you mind? I'd feel much better about the whole thing. I mean it's just not my fault, right? What do you want to do, live forever?

BOSWELL: No.

CELESTE: Exactly. So...will you forgive me?

BOSWELL: O K, alright, I forgive you.

CELESTE: Thank you. That's really very big of you. A lot of people, they don't want to say the words, you know what I mean? They want to hold on. They won't forgive me no matter what. Even though it's in their own best interest. Makes me feel like crap. Doesn't help with the whole low self-esteem thing, you know? So don't think I don't appreciate it.

BOSWELL: You're not going to stop watching me just because I forgave you, are you?

CELESTE: Oh nnnnno. Of course not. Don't be silly. I'll be right there with you. Oh, Sugar Smacks, I gotta get going. Pete gets all pissy if all the angels aren't in by ten.

BOSWELL: O K.

CELESTE: You're a nice guy. I'm gonna be sorry to see you go.

BOSWELL: But...Wait...I'm not...

CELESTE: NO! Of course not, quit being so darned paranoid. I'm just saying is all. Anyway thanks for forgiving me, I really do appreciate it.

BOSWELL: No problem.

(CELESTE snaps her fingers twice and exits. After a moment BOSWELL TWO enters.)

BOSWELL: What are you doing here?

BOSWELL TWO: I need to do more research. I wanted to watch you in action.

BOSWELL: How did you find me?

BOSWELL TWO: See...I'm good. I'm like a real-life Tracker. I can find people. I've been practicing. Watch this. "He's alive...I'll find him." Good, right?

BOSWELL: Yeah, sure. Oh, you were very good as Julius Caesar, by the way.

BOSWELL TWO: Oh, thanks, love to play that Caesar. But now I'm on to an even more challenging role—you. So tell me what you really think. Of this whole "Tracker" play I mean.

BOSWELL: It's good.

BOSWELL TWO: No, but I mean really. Because I'm trying to get it right. I want to capture your true essence. I want to be more you than you are.

BOSWELL: Well...I appreciate that, I'd like you to be more like me. I mean, I'm really not all that exciting. Its sort of a lonely life.

BOSWELL TWO: What? With all the adventure? You've got to be kidding. Look at this, we're here sitting on this stoop because...why exactly?

BOSWELL: I'm staking out that hotel. (He taps his watch and holds it to his ear.)

BOSWELL TWO: We are? See, that's exciting.

BOSWELL: No, actually it's pretty boring. That's what I'm trying to tell you. It's not like what you think. You work hard, you do your best. But it's a boring job, tough hours.

BOSWELL TWO: What are you talking about? You're a Tracker. You find people. You save people's lives.

BOSWELL: True...

BOSWELL TWO: Why are you a Tracker anyway? What drew you into this life?

BOSWELL: It's a long story.

BOSWELL TWO: Yeah?

BOSWELL: Yeah.

BOSWELL TWO: Sounds juicy.

BOSWELL: Let's just say I like the idea of being able to find everyone, but since I *can't*, I think your play should be a little more honest.

BOSWELL TWO: But you're so good at what you do, you're like a superhero. Who can't you find?

BOSWELL: Never mind. O K? Just...never mind.

BOSWELL TWO: Touchy, touchy. I don't think you fully understand how amazing you are.

BOSWELL: You just have the wrong impression.

BOSWELL TWO: No. You have the wrong impression.

BOSWELL: I think I would know.

BOSWELL TWO: I don't think so. I know who you are. I know what you mean as a symbol. I've done research. You could be a role model. And I'm going to be you. I'm going to show the people the real Boswell.

BOSWELL: I want you to show people the truth.

BOSWELL TWO: (*Overlapping*) In fact, the real Boswell doesn't even need to exist. When people get a load of my Boswell—the myth will become more real than life.

BOSWELL: Great. I can't wait. Look, do me a favor, will ya? I gotta check in with a quick phone call. I want you to keep your eye on the hotel. Like a real Tracker would.(*He exits.*)

(*Lights fade out on* BOSWELL TWO *and up on* KIKI.)

KIKI: We don't sleep together anymore. The triple touch makes things a little difficult. It doesn't happen all the time, but once is enough as I'm sure you can imagine. It's not that I don't love him—I do. My husband is a bit

eccentric, but he is a good man. Can you imagine? That poor Matthew
fellow. The triple touch is even worse for him. No wonder he's crazy.
I certainly hope Matthew doesn't find James. Oh, I wish Mr Boswell
would call with an update.

(The phone rings. In a separate area the lights reveal SIMONE, *who is whispering
a message. The phone rings a second time. The lights reveal in a separate area* JOE,
*who is passively polishing a napkin dispenser. The phone rings a third time, and the
lights reveal in a separate area* MR FARQUAR *on his knees. On either side of him
stand* MASON *and* DRAKE *with guns pointed at his head. The lights return to* KIKI
with a phone, and BOSWELL *with a phone sharing the same space.)*

KIKI: Kiki Farquar.

BOSWELL: Mrs Farquar, it's Boswell.

KIKI: Mr Boswell, thank goodness. Do you have any news?

BOSWELL: I'm just checking in. Where's Mr Farquar?

KIKI: He went to the corner to buy some dog food.

BOSWELL: You have a dog?

KIKI: No.

BOSWELL: Then why is he getting dog food?

KIKI: He...because he...

(The lights crossfade quickly to PAUL.)

PAUL: Bacon, Bacon, I know that smell. It's bacon, it's bacon. Look there's
the box...what does it say? *(Holds up box)* I CAN'T READ. *(He laughs
maniacally.)* That is the funniest God-damned commercial I have ever seen.
I CAN'T READ. Of course he can't read...he's a dog. *(He snacks occasionally
on the dog biscuits.)* I thought that I should ready my V C R to tape it the
next time I saw it but then I realized: No, I will simply buy the product.
They have more than earned my consumer dollars. They brought some
brightness and humor into my life. And so I will buy their product and
bring it into my home, and whenever I wish I will play the part of the
dog and say my punch line and have a very good time at it. And tomorrow,
of course, I'll buy the company.*(He enters his house.)* Hello, wife.

KIKI: Paul, you're just in time, it's Mr Boswell.

PAUL: Hello, Mr Boswell. *(He plays nervously with his ring.)* Give me some
good news.

BOSWELL: Well... I haven't found James. Yet. But I found Matthew.

PAUL: You haven't found James? You have to find him.

BOSWELL: Don't worry, "He's alive...I'll find him." Or something. I guess. Anyway, I found Matthew. I'm watching him to see if he'll lead me to James. I always find my man. Well...almost always.

PAUL: Keep me posted. Don't fail. Finding James is more important than you know.

(Lights crossfade back to BOSWELL TWO. CELESTE *enters.)*

BOSWELL TWO: What's going on?

CELESTE: Oh, you again. You still here?

BOSWELL TWO: Who are you?

CELESTE: Didn't we just go through this?

BOSWELL TWO: Are you an angel?

*(*CELESTE *takes a hard look at him.)*

CELESTE: Oh, Ffff...udgecicles. I'm sorry. I thought you were someone else. You're not one of mine. *(She waves her hand.)* Forget me. *(She exits.)*

(Slide:"End Creation, Crumble Worlds." BOSWELL *enters.)*

BOSWELL: I miss anything?

BOSWELL TWO: Nope.

BOSWELL: Good.

BOSWELL TWO: So, what are we doing outside this hotel?

BOSWELL: I'm staking out a guy named Matthew Farquar.

BOSWELL TWO: Why are we doing that?

BOSWELL: I'm trying to find his brother James.

BOSWELL TWO: So why aren't we staking out James?

BOSWELL: I can't find him, but I think Matthew will lead me to him.

BOSWELL TWO: You can't find him?

BOSWELL: I'll find him, somehow I'll find him. Other than Matthew I have no leads. Things aren't usually such a dead end.

BOSWELL TWO: How long have you been staking out the hotel?

BOSWELL: I'm not sure. *(He taps his watch and holds it to his ear.)* Time's starting to get all strange on me. I think we should go in and make sure he's still there.

BOSWELL TWO: How do we do that?

BOSWELL: We talk to the clerk.

BOSWELL TWO: Let me do it.

BOSWELL: You'll fuck it up.

BOSWELL TWO: I won't. I swear.

BOSWELL: Alright I'll give you a shot. But you fuck it up and I'm gonna send you straight back to play practice.

(They enter the hotel, where the CLERK is waiting.)

BOSWELL TWO: Hi, how are you today? Um, were looking for a guy named Matthew Farquar.

CLERK: Sorry, can't help you.

BOSWELL TWO: He can't help us.

BOSWELL: Tell the clerk you saw him check in.

BOSWELL TWO: I saw him check in..

CLERK: Sorry, pal.

BOSWELL TWO: It's...uh...very important that we talk to him.

CLERK: You got some identification?

BOSWELL TWO: *(To BOSWELL)* ...Do you have any identification? I have my Equity card.

CLERK: Can't help you without some identification. Many of our guests prefer a little anonymity.

BOSWELL: Here's our identification. *(He throws some money on the counter. The sound of a cash register ringing)*

CLERK: I'd have to check the guest register.

BOSWELL: Uh-huh.

CLERK: I'm not sure I have the authority to do that at this point in time.

(BOSWELL throws down some more money. The sound of a cash register ringing. The clerk looks in his book.)

CLERK: Nope. Not here.

BOSWELL TWO: Oh well.

BOSWELL: I saw him check in.

CLERK: No one checked in around that time. Look for yourself. *(Shows BOSWELL the book)*

BOSWELL: If a guest has the proper...credentials, could he check in without registering?

BOSWELL TWO: Good question.

CLERK: That's against the law, my friend.

BOSWELL: Right. Like I said. Look, I just want to know if he's here.

CLERK: Wish I could help you.

BOSWELL: Who takes out your garbage?

CLERK: What?

BOSWELL: Your dumpster. Who do you pay to empty it?

CLERK: Guy comes in here every week.

BOSWELL: And you pay him cash.

CLERK: Yeah...

BOSWELL: And do you know why you pay him cash? Because he does a lot more than empty your dumpster. He keeps your back watched and your shoes clean, understand?

CLERK: So?

BOSWELL: Do you even know the name of the gentleman who performs these acts of kindness for you?

CLERK: Mazotta. Something Mazotta.

BOSWELL: Danny Mazotta. Well, Mr Mazotta's wife was involved in some improprieties not too long ago and I provided him with some photographs that were very meaningful to him.

CLERK: So?

BOSWELL: So Mr Mazotta, as I'm sure you've observed, is a very grateful individual. He gets wind that the employees in this establishment are not as helpful as they could be, he might be prone to allow some of the more unsavory elements in the neighborhood access into your fine establishment. Understand? Now then...where is he?

CLERK: Matthew Farquar, huh? Yeah, he came in here alright. Never took a room, though. Smoked a cigarette, used the bathroom.

BOSWELL: You talk to him?

CLERK: Just small talk. We talked about the game, weather, you know.

BOSWELL: That's it?

CLERK: Oh, there was one thing he said.

BOSWELL: What was that?

CLERK: He looked me deep in the eye and he said:

"Finally Here, Day of Reckoning.
Garden of Eden, Garden of Blood.
Brother over Brother, Cain unto Abel.
Blink of an Eye.

End Creation, Crumble Worlds.
Death of Man, Death of God.
Stoppage of Time, Linkage of History.
Luscious Jumella.

Commence Peyton, Beginning of Time.
Commence Jaromir, End of Time.
Luscious Aclima.

Kabil and Habil.
Bula Cula Wula,
Sim Sala Bim."

BOSWELL TWO: He said that?

CLERK: Yep. Just like that.

BOSWELL: You didn't find that sort of odd?

CLERK: We get all types. Then he slipped out through the bathroom window.

BOSWELL TWO: Oldest trick in the book.

BOSWELL: Thanks for the tip. Shit!

(BOSWELL *and* BOSWELL TWO *exit the hotel.*)

BOSWELL TWO: Hey, maybe some day you'll tell me the Danny Mazola story. Sounds like great research material.

BOSWELL: Who?

BOSWELL TWO: You know, the guy with the wife and the pictures.

BOSWELL: He doesn't exist, I made him up.

(*The lights change and everyone freezes.* SIMONE *enters and whispers in* BOSWELL's *ear. Over the sound system we hear "Go to Joe's diner."* SIMONE *exits and the scene resumes.*)

BOSWELL: You go back to the theater, I've gotta go to the diner.

BOSWELL TWO: The diner? Why?

BOSWELL: I don't know. Call it a hunch. (*He exits*)

(BOSWELL TWO *hails* ABACAB's *taxi.*)

BOSWELL TWO: Taxi! Do you know where (*insert name of theater*) is?

ABACAB: Oh, I'm sorry, I thought you were someone else. I can't take you. (ABACAB *drives offstage without* BOSWELL TWO.)

BOSWELL TWO: Well..., looks like I'm walking. (*He starts to walk, then starts to adopt the "walk of a Tracker."*) Like a real Tracker would. (*He addresses the audience.*) You see, this is a really good gig for me. Another title role in a play. My agent said it would be great for my career. Things are looking up.

Last thing I did before Caesar was a dog food commercial. You know the one, with the dog running around smelling the bacon. I wasn't even in it though, just did the voice. The pay's good, but it's not "Acting", you know what I mean? Although I don't really see myself as an "actor", because I don't act. "Acting" is pretending. I don't do that. I inhabit my characters. It's like..., I have different sides to my personality. There are literally all these different people running around inside of me. And when I'm in a play it gives me a chance to release these other sides of myself. It's an incredible feeling. I don't know what I'd do without it.

(The lights crossfade to CELESTE *and* MATTHEW *on the stoop. Slide: "Three Into One.")*

CELESTE: Fry?

MATTHEW: What's going on.

CELESTE: I stopped time. You want a fry?

MATTHEW: Sure. *(He takes some fries.)* You get these for free?

CELESTE: I shouldn't take them but I do. Don't tell anyone O K? I could get in trouble. So tell me something, you think it's right to kill people?

MATTHEW: I'm a bad-mama-jama.

CELESTE: Yeah, yeah, I know.

MATTHEW: I'm the...

CELESTE: I know, the rock in the shoe with the pus and the piss and the uch and the blech. I know, but you're not answering my question. Do you think it's right to kill people?

MATTHEW: He who kills is alive. He who kills many is a conqueror.
He who kills all is God.

CELESTE: That's very poetic, thank you.

MATTHEW: I'm the salt in the wound.

CELESTE: I'm sure you are. Why do I always get stuck with the crazies? Listen to me. I'm your Guardian Angel. I'm here to look out for you. You shouldn't go around killing people.

MATTHEW: I shouldn't? *(He bites something off of his thumbnail.)*

CELESTE: No. How would you like it if someone killed you, huh? Do unto others and all that, you know what I mean? Besides, it would make things more difficult for me if I had to be constantly watching you, making sure you didn't kill one of my other clients. I got better things to do with my time, so just cut the shenanigans, will ya?

MATTHEW: I'm the baby who won't stop crying. I'm the job you didn't get, the name you can't remember, and the virus you don't know is growing inside you.

CELESTE: You must be a real treat at parties. Are you listening to me? Now, I want you to promise me you're not gonna kill anyone.

MATTHEW: I promise I'm not going to kill anyone.

CELESTE: Really?

MATTHEW: Sure.

CELESTE: Hey, wait a minute. Don't lie to me. You lie to me, I'm gonna make eternity very unpleasant for you. Are you lying?

MATTHEW: Of course I'm lying. I'm gonna find James and Paul and rip their heads off.

CELESTE: Why?

MATTHEW: To make only one of me.

CELESTE: There's only one of you, O K? I'm an angel, I know these things. There. Now you don't need to make anything.

MATTHEW: There's three of me, but I'll make three into one. Three. One. Even if it kills me.

CELESTE: There's only one of you, I swear. Only one.

(The lights crossfade to BRUTUS stabbing CAESAR.)

CAESAR: Et tu, Brute? Then fall Caesar.

(CAESAR dies. BRUTUS freezes. CAESAR gets up and addresses the audience.)

CAESAR: You know there's this one scene, Act Two, Scene Two, when Decius Brutus comes to take me to the Senate. And basically I tell him I ain't going. It's the ides of March, which the Soothsayer has warned me is trouble, my wife is having some fucked-up dreams about me spouting blood like a fountain, and basically I ask Decius Brutus to just tell the Senate to go on without me. But he convinces me to go with him and the rest as they say is...well, you know. My point is that with hindsight on my side it's awfully tempting every night to tell old Decius Brutus to fuck off. I mean I've done the play a million times, countless productions, and I know full well that if I go with him I'm history (pardon the pun). I mean, shit, the whole audience knows if I go with him I'm toast. And so just once I want to forget about what I'm supposed to say and convince old Decius that I'm not going and that he better get his sorry ass out of my chambers. But I can't. I mean I literally can't. And every night from the wings I hear those damn words "The fault, dear Brutus, lies not in our stars but in ourselves", and I think, yeah, that's right, no destiny. Take the matter into my own hands. All I have to do is say no. It's up to me. And then I hear myself saying "Give me my robe, for I will go", and next thing I know I got a knife sticking out of my heart. Every damn night. Over and over again like in a bad dream. There's gotta be a way out of this. There's just gotta be.

(Lights crossfade back to MATTHEW *sitting on the stoop.* SIMONE *enters.)*

SIMONE: Fry?

MATTHEW: Sure. *(He takes one and bites it.)* Ahhh! That's not a fry, it's a finger.

SIMONE: Teach you to bite your nails, you bad boy. *(She takes the finger and eats it.)* I've got all the half-chewed-up fingers from the bodies of my nervous former clients. Quite a collection. They make great snacks. Sure you don't want one?

MATTHEW: Mmm...yeah, I'm sure.

SIMONE: So my little psycho friend, you're not gonna listen to that Celeste bitch, are you?

MATTHEW: Who are you?

SIMONE: I'm Simone.

MATTHEW: Are you a Guardian Angel too?

SIMONE: Do I look like a Guardian Angel? I'm a Fallen Angel.

MATTHEW: Really? We have something in common then, 'cause I'm the fear of falling, a fallen arch, and your grandmother falling down the stairs.

SIMONE: I don't think you understand *(She raises her hands, and the lights and sound do something really dramatic and scary.)*

MATTHEW: Whoa. Cool.

SIMONE: Now look. Every Guardian Angel has a dark side. A fallen version of themselves. That's me. Get it? Now...you seem like a willing kind of a fella. Most people, they don't like to listen to angels like me. Or they like to listen, but they try not to. You on the other hand, seem like a willing audience.

MATTHEW: Sure.

SIMONE: Now look, you want to find James, right?

MATTHEW: Yeah, can you help me?

SIMONE: Of course I can. But you have to trust me.

MATTHEW: O K.

SIMONE: Now close your eyes. Use your instincts. Listen to the voice inside your head. Remember James. Remember what he thought, what he feared and what his passions were. Open your mind. What did he need? What would he do? What must he prove? Are you getting a picture?

MATTHEW: I think so.

SIMONE: Do you know where to start?

MATTHEW: I do.

SIMONE: Are you sure?

MATTHEW: I'm sure.

SIMONE: That's my boy. Now, are you ready to kick some butt?

MATTHEW: I am.

SIMONE: Are you gonna prove to the world that you're a psycho-freak from hell?

MATTHEW: I will!

SIMONE: Good boy. Now go out there and do some major killing.

MATTHEW: Hey, thanks, Simone. I really appreciate it. (*He exits and goes to the diner.*)

SIMONE: No problem. (*She laughs.*) He didn't know why, but Boswell felt a strong desire to go to the diner. Years as a Tracker had taught him not to ignore his instincts, and so that is where he headed. At least that's what he thought. (*She exits.*)

(BOSWELL *enters the diner where he finds* MATTHEW *sitting at the counter. He sits next to* MATTHEW, *and they acknowledge each other. The T V shows a frozen Knicks game. Slide:"A Distorted Apparition"*)

BOSWELL: Did you see the game last night?

MATTHEW: Very exciting, apparently. In the last three seconds, the lead changed eight times.

BOSWELL: All in three seconds? (*He taps his watch and holds it to his ear.*)

MATTHEW: It's amazing how much can happen in three seconds when it's at the very end. It can take so damn long too. I didn't see it though, just heard about it. Name's Matthew...

BOSWELL: I'm...

MATTHEW: Boswell.

BOSWELL: Yes. How did you...?

MATTHEW: Well, truth is, I just got outa the pen. You're famous up there. Lotta guys owe their time to you. Can't say you're very popular. Can I get your autograph? (*He hands* BOSWELL *a pen and a napkin.*)

BOSWELL: You want my autograph?

MATTHEW: Would you mind?

BOSWELL: Who should I make it out to?

MATTHEW: James Farquar.

BOSWELL: James?

MATTHEW: No, wait. That's wrong.

BOSWELL: To...?

MATTHEW: To...?

BOSWELL: Mmmmmm...

MATTHEW: Mmmmmm?

BOSWELL: Mmmmmm...

MATTHEW: mmmmMMMathew. To Matthew Farquar. *From* James Farquar to *Matthew Farquar.*

BOSWELL: What?

MATTHEW: Boswell!? Wait. Sorry. I mean Boswell. Sometimes I get so confused. From Boswell to Matthew.

BOSWELL: You sure?

MATTHEW: Yes. I'm sure.

(BOSWELL *signs the napkin.*)

BOSWELL: Here you go.

MATTHEW: Thanks. I really appreciate it.

BOSWELL: You said you were in prison. What were you in for?

MATTHEW: "What was I in for" or "what did I do"? (*He bites something off of his thumbnail.*)

BOSWELL: What did you do?

MATTHEW: Nothing. I was framed.

BOSWELL: Really?

MATTHEW: They said I broke all the toys. Truth is... I never touched the toys. James broke them all. He does the crime, I do the time. How do you like that?

BOSWELL: I'm sorry.

MATTHEW: Yeah? Why? Ever happen to you?

BOSWELL: I don't have a brother.

MATTHEW: Me neither.

BOSWELL: Oh. I thought James...

MATTHEW: He's not a brother, damnit! He's not! Stop saying that. He's another me. A third me. I can feel them out there. All the time.

BOSWELL: I'm sorry.

MATTHEW: It has to stop. It makes me crazy. I have to get rid of them.

BOSWELL: What if you get lonely without them?

MATTHEW: Lonely? Everyone's lonely. Aren't you lonely? Oh, no, of course not. You're a famous Tracker. You can find everyone...

BOSWELL: Not everyone...

MATTHEW: How can someone who can find people ever be lonely?

BOSWELL: I can be lonely.

MATTHEW: Why are you a Tracker, Mr Boswell? Who is it you're really looking for?

BOSWELL: I don't know. No one.

MATTHEW: Uh-huh.

BOSWELL: I'm not looking for anyone.

MATTHEW: How can one man tell such big lies to himself?

BOSWELL: What do you know about it? (Pause) Huh? Answer me. Answer me!

MATTHEW: I can't.

BOSWELL: Why not?

MATTHEW: I'm not here.

BOSWELL: You're not here?

MATTHEW: I'm not here. I'm here. (He touches BOSWELL's head.)

BOSWELL: Am I dreaming?

MATTHEW: I don't know. Pinch yourself.

(BOSWELL pinches himself.)

MATTHEW: Did you wake up?

BOSWELL: Sort of.

MATTHEW: And... (We hear the sound of distant wind chimes.)

BOSWELL: I'm sitting alone.

MATTHEW: I'm a distorted apparition.

BOSWELL: Am I even at the diner? Who are you?

MATTHEW: I am your sixth sense. I'm the ominous cloud on the horizon, the two-way mirror, and the feeling that it's coming.

BOSWELL: What?

MATTHEW: I'm a message. A warning.

BOSWELL: A warning about what?

MATTHEW: Beware the ides of March. *(He laughs.)* Just a joke. Beware of Joe's diner. *(He exits.)*

(KIKI appears in the diner.)

BOSWELL: A distorted apparition? A message. A warning.

KIKI: I saw you flirting with me.

BOSWELL: Oh, Jesus, you scared me. What are you doing here?

KIKI: In front of my own husband, you flirted with me.

BOSWELL: I didn't flirt with you. I didn't say a word.

KIKI: You're the strong silent type.

BOSWELL: Was I even there?

KIKI: How lonely does a man have to be to flirt with a woman in front of her own husband?

BOSWELL: How did you find me?

KIKI: You made eyes at me, Mr Boswell. You looked me in the eye and told me more about yourself in that one glance than most people tell me in a lifetime.

BOSWELL: You're a very attractive woman, Mrs Farquar.

KIKI: Hmmph. Beauty is in the eye of the beholder, isn't it?

BOSWELL: You're the kind of woman a man like me dreams about.

KIKI: Then I'll see you in your dreams.

(Blackout. Lights up on BOSWELL and the actor who plays CAESAR and BOSWELL TWO. Throughout the scene the actor keeps switching roles.)

BOSWELL: Where am I?

CAESAR: You're in Rome.

BOSWELL: I don't think so.

CAESAR: It's forty-four years before the birth of Christ, one thousand six hundred and eight years before the birth of Shakespeare, and you, my friend, are dressed terribly inappropriately.

BOSWELL: Whatever you say, pal.

BOSWELL TWO: You're right. You're not in Rome, you're onstage.

BOSWELL: Onstage?

BOSWELL TWO: You're alone. Onstage. You are the title character in a play about your life. It's the final act, you're naked, and you don't know any of your lines.

BOSWELL: I don't think I got your name.

CAESAR: I am Julius Caesar. Conqueror of Pompey and the title character of a play by William Shakespeare. Terrible play by the way, I am portrayed as a weakling and a braggart. Completely untrue to history. A horribly unfair legacy.

BOSWELL: Julius Caesar is dead.

BOSWELL TWO: So are you.

BOSWELL: I'm not dead. And neither are you. Who are you?

BOSWELL TWO: I'm Boswell. I'm you. You as the after-you. I'm the memory of you that will linger on. The part of you that is immortal.

BOSWELL: If you're me, who am I?

CAESAR: You are Decius Boswell. And you have come to take me to the Senate, where I will be rudely assassinated.

BOSWELL: I don't want to.

CAESAR: Well, I don't want you to either, but unfortunately we have no choice. So come on. Hail a cab and off we go.

BOSWELL: I'm dreaming, right?

BOSWELL TWO: It all gets confused in there. (Points to his head) Especially when you're down to your last second.

BOSWELL: My head hurts.

BOSWELL TWO: I'll bet it does. Have yourself a cup of coffee, you'll feel much better.

BOSWELL: Are you really me?

BOSWELL TWO: I'm really you.

BOSWELL: But there can't be two of me. There can't be two of me, or one of us has to die. How can you really be me?

BOSWELL TWO: Someone has to be.

(Blackout. The sound of a grandfather clock striking ten a little too quickly. Spotlight on the clock. The second hand moves another second. Lights crossfade to Madison Square Garden, where PAUL is eating from a dogfood box. KIKI sits next *to him. We hear the sounds of inspirational ballgame music. Slide: "Black, Bitter Death")*

PAUL: "Said Go New York, Go New York, Go."

KIKI: "Go New York, Go New York, Go."

PAUL: "Let's go Knicks."

KIKI: "Let's go Knicks."

PAUL: De-Fense.

KIKI: De-Fense.

PAUL: De-Fense.

KIKI: De-Fense.

PAUL: Hmmm. *(He licks his chops and plays with his ring.)*

KIKI: What's the matter?

PAUL: What's that?

KIKI: What?

PAUL: That taste? That's not bacon, that's...coffee.

KIKI: Coffee?

PAUL: The taste of coffee. Someone's having coffee. Oh, for Christ's sake. Matthew? Are you drinking coffee?

KIKI: Matthew?

PAUL: James? Who's having their coffee? *(He licks his chops.)* Hmmm? Blech. No sugar. I hate that. Put some sugar in there, damn it! Like drinking a cup of black, bitter death. Brrring. Brrring.

KIKI: Paul, are you alright?

PAUL: Hmmm? What's that ringing? Brrring. Hello? What's that ringing?

KIKI: Ringing?

PAUL: Oh, God, look out...

KIKI: What?

PAUL: Look out, look out. AAAArrRRgHHhh? Oh, my head.

KIKI: Paul?

PAUL: I've killed a man, taken a life. I'm dead too. I'm the killer and the killed. AAarhGghr. I'll never know who wins this game. AAarhGghr. Ringing, seconds, angels, Caesar. I've been betrayed. Brutus? Joe? AAarhGghr. I love my wife. My wife, goodbye. AAarhGghr. Three different

memories all as one. All at once. Embrace death. My true self. AAarhGghr.
(He dies.)

KIKI: Oh, my god! My husband's been murdered!

(Blackout. Slide:"Constinct". CELESTE has replaced KIKI.)

CELESTE: Fry?

PAUL: Are they fried in animal fat?

CELESTE: Uh-huh.

PAUL: Then I probably shouldn't.

CELESTE: Why not?

PAUL: It's not good for you.

CELESTE: Are you kidding?... Hello. You're dead, buddy.

PAUL: I am? Oh, that's right, I keep forgetting. Is that common at first?
To forget you're dead?

CELESTE: Quite common, actually.

PAUL: Let me ask you something, what kind of a world is it when your own
brother strikes you down dead in the middle of a diner? I mean, what's the
matter with this world? I tried to protect myself, did I not? And where,
by the way, were you?

CELESTE: Hey, don't try and pin this on me, I did the best I could.

PAUL: Least you could have done was guard me a little better, you are my
Guardian Angel, are you not?

CELESTE: *Was* your Guardian Angel.

PAUL: Oh...right. Sorry. It's gonna take some time getting used to referring
to myself in the past tense.

CELESTE: Well, luckily, time is one thing we have plenty of around here.

PAUL: So we do. How do Guardian Angels do their guarding anyway?
Do you swoop down and deflect oncoming cars out of the way and stuff
like that?

CELESTE: Only when things get desperate. Usually we use something we call
"constinct".

PAUL: "Constinct"?

CELESTE: You betcha. It's a cross between conscience and instinct.
It's like...you know when you hear a voice in your head telling you
to do something?

PAUL: Yes.

CELESTE: Like maybe it's your moral side telling you to do something because it seems right, or maybe you just feel you should do something even though you don't know why? Well, that's us. We write those little inner monologues and plop em down inside your thoughts.

PAUL: Do I get to be a Guardian Angel?

CELESTE: Only time will tell.

PAUL: Does it get boring? I mean, am I gonna like death?

CELESTE: Well, technically, you're not dead yet.

PAUL: I'm not?

CELESTE: We've got time stopped. There's still one thing you have to do before we get time rolling again.

PAUL: What's that?

CELESTE: Deliver your message.

(Blackout. The lights crossfade to a SOOTHSAYER who stands alone on the street. CAESAR and BRUTUS come walking by.)

SOOTHSAYER: Caesar!

CAESAR: Ha! Who calls? Cry "Caesar!" Speak. Caesar is turned to hear.

SOOTHSAYER: Beware the ides of March.

CAESAR: What man is that?

BRUTUS: A soothsayer bids you beware the ides of March.

CAESAR: Set him before me; let me see his face.

BRUTUS: Fellow, look upon Caesar.

CAESAR: What sayst thou to me now? Speak once again.

SOOTHSAYER: Beware the ides of March.

CAESAR: He is a dreamer. Let us leave him.

(CAESAR and BRUTUS continue walking past the SOOTHSAYER. They freeze. The lights come up on JOE in the diner.)

JOE: Guy walks into the diner, looks exactly like Bos. I mean exactly. Tells me he's looking for his long lost brother or something and do I know where Bos might be? Guy looks like trouble so I buy a little time, make some crack about "What, does finding people run in your family?" But he doesn't laugh. Guy takes himself very seriously. Keeps telling me he's my nightmare, my death, and my... something else, I don't know. So, sure, I tell him when Bos is likely to be around, you know? I mean the guy looks just like him, they have to be related. I thought...I don't know, maybe Bos would be happy to see him or something. I didn't know he was gonna...I mean he didn't *tell* me. *(Pause)* He said he would hurt my wife if I didn't help him, alright? He said he could find her and that he would... Look, I didn't actually *do* anything. He would've found Bos anyway even if I hadn't told him. He would have. I did not betray my friend. Just don't judge me, alright? Don't judge me, because I didn't do anything you wouldn't have done.

(JOE exits and runs into BRUTUS. BRUTUS, CAESAR, and JOE exit. BOSWELL enters in pursuit of a cab.)

BOSWELL: Taxi!

SOOTHSAYER: Boswell?

BOSWELL: Sorry, I don't have any change.

SOOTHSAYER: Boswell!!

BOSWELL: Huh? Are you talking to me? Who are you?

SOOTHSAYER: I am a soothsayer. Read this.

(BOSWELL looks at the paper.)

BOSWELL: I'm sorry, I can't read.

SOOTHSAYER: Can't read? I'll read it to you. "Beware of Joe's diner".

BOSWELL: I can't read?

(Slide:"Turbo Booty Booster." BOSWELL enters ABACAB's taxi.)

BOSWELL: Taxi! You know where Joe's diner is?

ABACAB: Get in. *(She examines him in the rearview mirror.)* You look like you've seen better days.

BOSWELL: Excuse me? *(He taps his watch and holds it to his ear.)*

ABACAB: There I go stickin' my nose in other people's business again. I'm sorry. I'm Abacab.

BOSWELL: Abacab?

ABACAB: Real name's Jane. Jane Abbey, but when I started driving, they called me Abbey-cabbie. Now I'm just Abacab. You can call me Jane if you prefer.

BOSWELL: Uh-huh, O K. Are you wearing a wedding dress?

ABACAB: Sure am.

BOSWELL: Are you getting married?

ABACAB: Nooooo. I skipped out on that jerk. Left him at the altar years ago.

BOSWELL: Why?

ABACAB: He was a lying sack of shit. Caught him with another woman.
He said it wasn't him. I mean he said it was him but that he was possessed
by pod people like in that movie, so it wasn't really like it was him.
You believe that? Stupid me said I'd marry him anyway. But then there
I was, literally marching down the aisle of my destiny. And I thought:
"Its over, there's nothing I can do. I chose this path, and I must face the
consequences." And then I thought: "Wait. There is no destiny. Take the
matter into my own hands. All I have to do is say no", and I hightailed it
on out of there.

BOSWELL: And then after you left this guy at the altar you became a cab
driver?

ABACAB: Sure did. Best job in the world. Get to take people wherever they
want to go. And I do mean wherever.

(ABACAB *steps hard on the accelerator, and the lights and sound do whatever the
lights and sound did when "The Millennium Falcon" went into hyperspace.*)

BOSWELL: Whoa. Uh, slow down, O K?

ABACAB: Don't worry. Nothing can touch us at warp speed.

(*The sound of a car horn careening out of the way.*)

ABACAB: Imagine my good fortune. Eleven thousand cabs in this city and I
get the one with the hyperdrive. I do have the luck of the saints. So what do
you say...where should we go?

BOSWELL: Just to Joe's diner, that's as far as I need to go, really.

ABACAB: Oh, come on. We got the turbo-booty-boosters working for us.
We can go anywhere we want. We can go so damn fast we could cheat time.
Beat her at her own game. How can you say no to an offer like that?

BOSWELL: Jane... stop this crazy thing.

ABACAB: Oh, come on, live a little. How 'bout we go backwards? Make time
do it over for us again. You wanna see yourself as a little tyke?

BOSWELL: I can't, I don't remember my childhood very well.

ABACAB: Perfect. All the more reason. Here we go. Nineties... Clinton
elected. Eighties... stock market crash. Seventies... Steve Miller band.
Mets win the World Series? Whoa, Nelly.

(ABACAB *slams on the brakes. We hear the sound of shattering glass, and then the
lights and sound are restored.*)

ABACAB: Goddamn it. Always hit them brakes too hard. Gonna have to
get me a new windshield now. It's always something. Well, what are you
waiting for? Step on out and take a look.

(BOSWELL *exits the cab and steps into a scene between* MR FARQUAR *and young* JAMES. ABACAB *exits.*)

FARQUAR: I can't keep you anymore, do you understand?

JAMES: Yes.

FARQUAR: Where you're going is nice. Nicer than what I can give you. I'm in trouble, and I just can't keep you kids with me, you understand?

JAMES: Yes.

FARQUAR: But maybe some day we'll meet up, huh? In a world better than this one. Wouldn't that be good, James?

JAMES: Yes.

FARQUAR: Now look, uh, I gotta go, but that nice foster-home lady we met with is gonna meet you here and she's gonna bring you someplace real special where you're gonna have a good Mommy and Daddy.

JAMES: Maybe I can see you later.

FARQUAR: No, James, we're not gonna see each other again. Not in this life.

JAMES: When I get to be a grown-up, I'll look for you, and I'll find you, and then we'll be together again.

FARQUAR: I wouldn't look too hard.

JAMES: I'll find you, Daddy, I will.

FARQUAR: Whatever you say, buddy. (*We hear a whistle from offstage.*) Now listen, Daddy has to go, O K, pal?

JAMES: O K. (*Pause*) Daddy?

FARQUAR: Yeah?

JAMES: Can I bring Paul and Matthew with me?

FARQUAR: Come on now, James, don't start with me.

JAMES: Please?

FARQUAR: How many times do we have to go through this?

JAMES: Please, Daddy?

FARQUAR: James, you three can't be together anymore. You need to go away from all this and forget about this life.

JAMES: If I can't have a Mommy, and now I can't even have a Daddy, can't I please at least take my brothers with me? Please?

FARQUAR: You're gonna have a Daddy, a good Daddy.

(MASON *and* DRAKE *enter.*)

MASON: Come on, let's go. Time's up.

FARQUAR: You be a big strong boy for me, O K? O K, James? You just forget about your brothers and get on with your new life.

JAMES: O K, Daddy.

FARQUAR: And remember, whatever happens, I'll always care about you. *(He leaves with MASON and DRAKE. The lights change.)*

CELESTE: You know, it's interesting, they say that when you die, your life flashes before your eyes. But that assumes that your "life" is a series of images immutably fixed in your brain. And that is not at all the nature of memory. Memory flows like sand down a wall. And as the oxygen supply to the brain begins to diminish, the images get fuzzy and the synapses pop. Whole worlds crumble and reform in the blink of an eye. Act Three. Second Three.

(BOSWELL enters the diner. The T V is showing a Knicks game. Slide:"Narratives Formed From Dust.")

BOSWELL: Hey, Joe. Gimme a coffee, will ya?

JOE: Comin' up, Bos. *(Referring to the T V)* Oh, for Christ's sake.

(BOSWELL taps his watch and holds it to his ear.)

JOE: Ridiculous game. Refs won't cut Ewing any slack. Keeps getting called for "three seconds."

BOSWELL: Tough break. I usually like to stay home when the Knicks play. Watch the game. Sometimes I don't even pay attention to what's going on, I just like to watch.

JOE: Yup.

BOSWELL: Had to be at the theater tonight, though.

JOE: Yeah?

BOSWELL: New play they're doing called "Tracker". Based loosely on my experiences you know?

JOE: You're shittin' me. Congratulations.

BOSWELL: Yeah. Thanks. They're doing a good job. I just wish they'd be a little more faithful to who I truly am.

JOE: Pfff.

BOSWELL: What?

JOE: Who among us knows who he truly is?

(BOSWELL taps his watch and holds it to his ear.)

JOE: Watch stop?

BOSWELL: My watch, time, everything. I don't know. How's Alice?

JOE: She's fine...thanks.

BOSWELL: Glad to hear it. (*He taps his watch and holds it to his ear.*)

JOE: Supposed to snow tonight, you hear that?

BOSWELL: Snow? It's the middle of September.

JOE: Greenhouse effect. No ozone. World's coming to an end.

(*It begins to snow golden snow.*)

JOE: Earthquake'll hit California, half the state'll fall into the ocean. Whole world's crumbling. What can you do?

BOSWELL: Nothing, I guess.

JOE: There's a law of diminishing returns or something on disaster, though.

(BOSWELL *notices a pinspot or something crawling on the counter like a cockroach.*)

BOSWELL: What's that?

JOE: You know, like as far as feeling tragedy is concerned. It's, like, for us five million dead in China equals five thousand dead in California equals fifty dead in New York equals someone killed your brother.

(*The pinspot is becoming all-absorbing of* BOSWELL's *attention.* MATTHEW *enters the diner unseen by* BOSWELL *but seen by* JOE. *He sneaks up behind* BOSWELL.)

BOSWELL: What?

JOE: Any of which could happen at anytime.

BOSWELL: Uh-huh.

JOE: The whole world's turning to shit in the blink of an eye. It's unbelievable. Anything can get you. One second you're just sitting there, next thing you know....

(JOE *snaps his fingers.* MATTHEW *hits* BOSWELL *over the head with a pipe. We hear the sound of glass shattering. Blackout. The sound of a grandfather clock striking ten at speed.*)

CELESTE: At the stroke of ten a man who could barely even remember who he truly is was suddenly struck from behind with a pipe to the head. He was engulfed by confusion. Fantasies becoming memories as thoughts and dreams became realities.

(*Faint blue light comes up just enough so we can see but not enough to suggest the lights have returned. The Knicks game is frozen.* PAUL *is where* JOE *was.* MATTHEW *is hovering about.*)

BOSWELL: What's happening to me?

PAUL: You failed. I failed. I don't know.

BOSWELL: You found James?

MATTHEW: Yes.

BOSWELL: Is James dead?

PAUL: One more second.

BOSWELL: Is James me?

PAUL: We're brothers.

BOSWELL: What are you doing here?

PAUL: I'm delivering a message. I'm actually sitting in the garden.

BOSWELL: What garden?

PAUL: Madison Square Garden. Courtside. What a way to go. I can see the headlines. Paul Farquar, eccentric billionaire, dead of a crushed skull. No assailant found. Nineteen thousand witnesses and no one saw a thing. In a related story, two found dead in a diner. Both from crushed skulls.

MATTHEW: I didn't know.

PAUL: You know now.

BOSWELL: So what happens now?

PAUL: No matter what your destiny, it really only consists of a single moment, the moment in which you know once and for all who you truly are. It's time for you to go. Snap, twitch, and blink.

(He snaps his fingers twice. The lights go out. We are in complete darkness.)

VOICE OF BOSWELL: What? Paul? What? What do you mean? Paul? Speak to me!

VOICE OF PAUL: Snap, twitch, and blink, and it'll all be over. Snap. Twitch. And blink. Worlds crumble in the blink of an eye.

(We hear the sound of two snaps. The lights come up to reveal BOSWELL alone in the diner. CELESTE begins to sweep up the golden snow.)

BOSWELL: Celeste...?

CELESTE: What do you feel?

BOSWELL: I can feel my head cracking and parts of my skull crumbling away.

CELESTE: It's O K. Tell me what else.

BOSWELL: I hear a ringing in my head. Maybe it's the phone or just the clock striking ten.

CELESTE: You only have three seconds. Tell yourself your story.

(MATTHEW and PAUL are revealed in a separate area.)

BOSWELL: I'm looking into my killer's eyes. Christ it's like looking into a mirror. This can't be real, it must be a part of the play. The play about me? The Caesar play?

(CAESAR *appears is a separate area.*)

CELESTE: Narratives formed from dust.

(JOE *appears behind the counter, polishing something.*)

BOSWELL: Joe? Why are you just standing there? Joe? Help me. Please.

(MASON *and* DRAKE *are revealed is a separate area with guns pointed at* FARQUAR's *head.*)

BOSWELL: My father. I remember. He's dead. My brothers? What have I been looking for?... My true self. My heart is slowing down. Stopping.

(ABACAB *enters.*)

ABACAB: Get in.

CELESTE: Let go.

BOSWELL: I'm dead.

(CELESTE *throws a handful of snow into the air. The lights fade down to the clock, which ticks a third and final second. Blackout*)

END OF PLAY

THE HANDLESS MAIDEN

ORIGINAL PRODUCTION

THE HANDLESS MAIDEN was first presented by the adobe theatre company, opening on 25 February 1998. The cast and creative contributors were:

ERIC/MERLE .... Vin Knight
ANN/CRONEY .... Lia Yang
MAIDEN/JULIE/LISA .... Molly Renfroe
DAVE/GARDENER/BARTENDER .... Matthew Aibel
MILLER'S WIFE/MESSENGER .... Janice O'Rourke
MILLER/MOE .... Arthur Aulisi
DEVIL/MAX .... Christopher Marobella
KING/PETER .... Bryan Webster

Director .... Damon Kiely
Sets .... Steven Capone
Lighting .... Christien Methot
Costumes .... Carol Bailey
Sound .... Chris Todd
Original music .... Michael Garin

CHARACTERS

Note: The actors play more than one character. While it should be clear that it is the same actor, something should be done to make sure there is no confusion that it might be the same character, i.e., distinct costumes.

ERIC/MERLE
ANN/CRONEY
MAIDEN/JULIE/LISA
DAVE/GARDENER/BARTENDER
MILLER'S WIFE/MESSENGER
MILLER/MOE
DEVIL/MAX
KING/PETER

MUSIC

When the adobe theatre company first presented the play in February 1998, we added some musical numbers that were written and arranged by Michael Garin. While they add a nice element of theatricality and I highly recommend using them, the play can be done without music. This script presents Michael's lyrics intact as well as ways to play the scenes without the songs. Should any producer desire to present the play with the music, they should contact Michael Garin for permission through Mitch Douglas at I C M, 40 W 57th St, New York, NY 10019, 212-556-5600. If the music is not used, the "Once upon a time's" at the top of scenes one, two, and three should be spoken rather than sung as indicated.

ACT ONE

(Prologue: Lights on ERIC and ANN on opposite sides of the stage, driving. They each have a faraway look in their eyes. Lights up on the MAIDEN. ANN sings:)

ANN: Once upon a time, a few weeks ago, in a faraway kingdom called New York City...

Scene One

(ANN and DAVE's. Dinner. An open bottle of wine)

ANN: O K, what about "Max"?

DAVE: No, God, I hate the name Max. I had an uncle Max who used to, you know the type, used to throw me in the pool when I was a little kid and scream, "It's the only way to learn how to swim, kick, you little twerp, kick for your life."

ANN: God, you have a problem with every single name.

DAVE: Well, what is with this name game all of a sudden? You're not pregnant?

ANN: Don't you think we should have a name in mind?

DAVE: Sure. But why now? Answer my question.

ANN: No, I'm not pregnant.

DAVE: So, then? Hey, you were the one, if I recall correctly, who said she wanted to be made partner first....

ANN: Yes...

DAVE: ...wanted more stability in our lives.

ANN: ...you recall correctly, counselor, that is what I said, but...

DAVE: Well, alright then. We stay on the plan. One of us gets made partner. Probably me. Then we start thinking family.

ANN: Well..., I have some interesting news.

DAVE: Yes?

ANN: Jacobson called me into his office today.

DAVE: Uh-huh?

ANN: They want to make me partner.

DAVE: Are you serious?

ANN: That's what he said.

DAVE: Why didn't you tell me?

ANN: I did just tell you.

DAVE: Ann, that's fantastic.

ANN: Youngest partner in the firm's history. First woman. Straight track to blah blah blah and all the way up.

DAVE: That's incredible. Why aren't you jumping up and down? We should be out celebrating. If you'd called me, I would've made a reservation. We could be out instead of here eating this.

ANN: I thought you liked this.

DAVE: I do. Mmmm.

ANN: Don't make me come over there and tickle you.

DAVE: No, that would be very undignified for a partner. A New Partner? And so now it's time to start thinking baby names. Well, I guess I owe you a hundred dollars.

ANN: For what?

DAVE: You don't remember?

ANN: Remember what?

DAVE: I guess I shouldn't have brought it up, then. Could've saved a hundred dollars. You really don't remember the bet we made?

ANN: Mmm-mmm.

DAVE: Junior year. Your dorm room. We were pretty drunk, I guess. It was after Sasha's homecoming bash, and you bet me a hundred dollars that you'd make partner before I would. You had absolutely no doubt you'd win. Even though you swore you'd only do it for the good guys and I could do it for anyone. And you were right. You win. (*He takes a hundred-dollar bill out of his wallet and puts it on the table.*)

ANN: You can keep the money, Dave.

DAVE: No, no. A bet's a bet. You win fair and square. (*He writes something on the bill in big letters.*)

ANN: I didn't say yes. (*Pause*)

DAVE: Why?

ANN: I didn't say no. But I didn't say yes. I said I'd have to talk it over with my husband.

DAVE: Well, I'm touched. Thank you very much. But. So. We talked about it. Don't be ridiculous. Of course I want you to take it. It's what you've always wanted.

ANN: Well, I'm not sure it's what I still want. Things change.

DAVE: You want me to talk you out of it? Why would you possibly want to say no?

ANN: Maybe I want to start a family.

DAVE: We're going to start a family. This is what we've been waiting for.

ANN: But it makes no sense. How are we going to start a family if I'm a partner? What the hell were we thinking?

DAVE: This is a dream come true. You can't start making up excuses to keep yourself from succeeding.

ANN: Can't I just change my mind?

DAVE: We have a plan. It's a good plan.

ANN: We can't change the plan?

DAVE: It's what we've agreed on for our lives. Don't you want that?

ANN: I don't know.

DAVE: Well, if you rejected the offer, what would you want to do?

ANN: I don't know. Quit?

DAVE: What? Jacobson is offering you the opportunity of a lifetime.

ANN: You're not listening to me.

DAVE: No, you're not listening to yourself. I know it's scary to get what you want but, trust me, once you settle into it, you'll see. You'll get the cases you want, you'll get respect. And the rest of our plan will follow.

ANN: How can I know that for sure?

DAVE: I guarantee it. "In times of crisis, always do what you said you would do when you were thinking..."

ANN: Rationally.

DAVE: This is a hell of an offer. It'll take more work, but it'll be worth it, you know that.

ANN: Maybe you're right.

DAVE: We have a good plan. We have a good life.

ANN: I know. You think I just freaked?

DAVE: Yes.

ANN: I guess I got scared.

DAVE: I know, honey.

ANN: Do you think I'm crazy?

DAVE: No. Of course not.

ANN: Alright. I'll do it. *(She takes the hundred-dollar bill and looks at what* DAVE *wrote.)* "For the true winner." Cute.

DAVE: Oh, Ann. I am so proud of you. *(He pours the remainder of the wine into her glass and then his.)* Tomorrow night I'll take you out and we'll celebrate the next phase of our life together.

(They clink glasses and drink.)

Scene Two

*(*ERIC *in* ERIC *and* JULIE's *living room.* ERIC *sings:)*

ERIC: Once upon a time, a few weeks ago, in a faraway kingdom called Seattle.

*(*JULIE *enters.)*

JULIE: Hi, honey.

ERIC: Welcome home. Did you have a good day?

JULIE: They're all brats.

ERIC: I know, sweetie.

JULIE: Why can't kids listen anymore? Is that so much to ask? Sit. Listen. Don't throw anything. Don't kill anybody. And just maybe in the process you might learn something.

ERIC: Come here.

(They kiss.)

ERIC: Give me your feet.

(She takes off her shoes, and he rubs her feet.)

JULIE: What did you do today?

ERIC: Well...I've got a lot to fill you in on.

JULIE: Yes?

ERIC: First of all, I went to confirm our registry list. Those people at Williams Sonoma are a nightmare. I was forced to change around a couple of your suggestions, but I think you're going to be very happy.

JULIE: Like what?

ERIC: Nothing major. Only improvements.

JULIE: Oh. O K.

ERIC: Next. I talked to the photographer.

JULIE: And?

ERIC: He agreed with me. We should definitely do the video.

JULIE: You don't think the photos are enough?

ERIC: There's no need for modesty.

JULIE: I just think video cameras are so intrusive. I don't want someone shining bright lights on me through the whole thing.

ERIC: It's totally worth it. I mean you only get a special day like this once in your life and I want everything to be perfect. And I want to remember it perfectly and be able to show it to our kids perfectly.

JULIE: So it has to be on video?

ERIC: You're going to look so beautiful in my mother's dress, and I want it all captured properly. I mean, don't you wish you had a video of your parent's wedding? The last thing we want is to regret not doing it.

JULIE: Alright, if you really think it's worth it, go ahead.

ERIC: That's what I told him. So we're all set.

JULIE: Eric?

ERIC: Yeah?

JULIE: You know how much I appreciate all the work you're doing on the preparations and everything.

ERIC: Not a problem.

JULIE: Well. Thank you. But, and...you know I'm really busy so it's hard for me to put all that work in.

ERIC: I completely understand.

JULIE: But I have to tell you. I mean, since I was a little girl you know, I've had certain visions of how it would be. And, I just want to make sure that I'm included. Does that make sense?

ERIC: Of course. I mean, me too. I have very specific ideas of what our wedding should be. But we've talked, haven't we? We've agreed.

JULIE: Yes, it's just...

ERIC: Very traditional. The whole nine yards. You want that too, don't you?

JULIE: I do...

ERIC: Because I know I do.

JULIE: It's just that sometimes you can be a little overbearing.

ERIC: I can...? I don't mean to be.

JULIE: No. I know. Of course you don't. It's just that I think sometimes you go and make decisions without really consulting me, and I just...it doesn't feel right.

ERIC: About the video?

JULIE: No, it's more of a general thing.

ERIC: I can stop, Julie. Back off I mean.

JULIE: I don't....

ERIC: But I mean, like you said, you don't really have the time....

JULIE: I'm not looking for a solution...

ERIC: And someone has to take care of these things.

JULIE: I know.

ERIC: Perfect example: Your mother called. She needs to invite more people, and is that O K?

JULIE: Who now?

ERIC: Apparently you have an Uncle Phil?

JULIE: I do?

ERIC: Great uncle? Beats me.

JULIE: I've never even met these people.

ERIC: She's your mother, Julie. You weren't here. Someone has to take care of these things.

JULIE: I'm just telling you how I feel.

ERIC: And...O K, well, what can I do to make it better?

JULIE: I don't know.

ERIC: Well...how can I give you want you want if you can't tell me what that is?

JULIE: You don't have to give me what I want all the time. I'm a big girl. You're so eager to please me you...sometimes just, I don't know.

ERIC: No. I what?

JULIE: You treat me like a princess, not a human being. You want so much to make this a perfect "event" up here, that you pay no attention to the "us" down here, and I don't know what that is, what that's about.

ERIC: I'm sorry.

JULIE: You try to make me happy, but then you keep me out of everything. Your eyes are like these impenetrable walls that I can never see through. I never know what you're thinking. I mean, I don't think you do it on purpose....

ERIC: No.

JULIE: But I just thought I should tell you how I felt.

ERIC: No, I'm glad you did. Believe me. It's not easy. I know. And I'm glad you could tell me.

JULIE: I love you, you know?

ERIC: I know. Of course... I love you too.

Scene Three

(MILLER's *house. She sings: Note: when we are in the fairy tale, production values and acting style are more cartoonlike. Not naturalistic.*)

MILLER'S WIFE: Once upon a time, a few weeks ago, in a magical kingdom far far away... (*She discovers some papers. Looks at them*) Oh my god! Jumping Jehosafers. Ooooh. This is terrible. Giuseppe. Giuseppe, come in here this instant. Giuseppe, I know you can hear me. Come in here this instant!

(MILLER *enters.*)

MILLER: Yes, my sweet darling wife. What is it? (*She points to the papers.*) Oh no. You should not look at those. You do not need to concern yourself with our financial matters.

MILLER'S WIFE: Financial matters? What financial matters? You have to have finances to have financial matters. According to this we're broke. Bust. Kaplooey.

MILLER: A woman does not need to concern herself with the accounting. That's a man's job.

MILLER'S WIFE: Man's job my fairy-tale ass. What kind of sexist nonsense is that? I'm tired of all this blatant sexism.

MILLER: What sexism?

MILLER'S WIFE: What sexism? What sexism? What's your name?

MILLER: Why, of course you know my name. You are my wife. My name is Guiseppe Egoist Libidinas Miller.

MILLER'S WIFE: And what's my name?

MILLER: Your name? Why. Your name is...Miller's Wife.

MILLER'S WIFE: Ah-ha. My point exactly. I don't even get a name. Wait? WHOA? Whhhooohhooohhoo. I am having a prophecy. Stand back. I am prophesizing. Mmmmmmnnn—Centuries from now in a faraway kingdom called New York City *(Insert name of city where show is performing)*. In a small theatre called the Ohio *(Insert name of theatre)*. A place with uncomfortable seating *(Insert own comically disparaging remark)*. This point will be uncovered, and young women will feel empowered. Yes. Go my soul sisters of the future. Learn from my plight and be strengthened. Sing. Sing the songs of Woman! *(The trance breaks.)* Whew. Oh. O K. Where were we?

MILLER: What has your prophecy to do with our household finances, my sweet and loving wife?

MILLER'S WIFE: Oh, right, the finances. You can't keep the finances. We're down to our last gold coin.

MILLER: Pshaw. Come now. Things have not gotten so bad. Can you really think we are down to our last gold coin?

MILLER'S WIFE: *(Pulling out a gold coin)* I have one gold coin. What've you got?

(MILLER sheepishly turns his pockets inside out.)

MILLER'S WIFE: Exactly.

MILLER: Well, we may not have but one gold coin...but we have other things.

MILLER'S WIFE: Like what?

MILLER: Like our love for each other.

MILLER'S WIFE: That and fifty ducats'll get me a frozen mochaccino, you know what I'm saying?

MILLER: Oh, a frozen mochaccino costs way more than fifty ducats.

MILLER'S WIFE: My point is, we have nothing.

MILLER: We have our apple tree...

MILLER'S WIFE: Giuseppe...

MILLER: Our abundant, flowing apple tree in the backyard.

MILLER'S WIFE: Giuseppe, I'm serious. This is terrible. What are we going to do?

MILLER: I don't know my darling. I tried to keep it from you. I didn't want you to worry. I've tried to make the business work, but times are hard. I can't seem to make ends meet.

MILLER'S WIFE: But what about the mill?

MILLER: The mill is not milling.

MILLER'S WIFE: The mill is not milling?

MILLER: The mill is not milling. The churn is not churning.

MILLER'S WIFE: Ooh. Things are worse than I thought. But don't worry, my sweet. We will find a way to get by.

MILLER: Yes, but how?

MILLER'S WIFE: Perhaps you should go into the forest and chop some wood.

MILLER: Chop some wood? What sort of a cockamamey idea is that? How is chopping some wood going to help our financial troubles?

(MILLER'S WIFE *bursts into song:*)

MILLER'S WIFE: When times are tough and money's low
As even fairy tales sometimes go
Just grab an ax and head out for the woods.

Forget your fortune dwindling
Go out and get some kindling
And show 'em all you've really got the goods.

You gotta chop chop chop chop chop chop down a tree
There'll be lots of wood for you and for me.

A bundle of faggots and lots of bark.
With enough left over for Noah's ark

You gotta chop chop chop chop chop chop down a tree.
You gotta chop chop chop chop chop chop down a tree.

Timber!

(*If the song is not used, insert the next line for* MILLER'S WIFE *instead.*)

MILLER'S WIFE: Well. It seems like the sort of thing one might do in a situation like this. (*Pause*) If one lived in a fairy tale.

MILLER: Alright, my darling wife. I am sure you are right. I will go to the forest and chop some wood.

MILLER'S WIFE: Be safe, my font of joy. And be home before dark.

MILLER: Yes, dear. (*He exits.*)

MILLER'S WIFE: Oh boy. Are we fucked.

(MILLER'S WIFE *exits.* MILLER *reenters.*)

MILLER: Well, here I am in the woods. I've got my trusty ax. Guess there's nothing to do but start chopping some wood.

(*He begins to chop some wood. From out of the shadows steps a dark, shadowy figure.*)

DEVIL: Hello, Giuseppe Egoist Libidinas Miller.

MILLER: Hello? Who is that? Do I know you?

DEVIL: Never you mind. I know you. That is all that's important. I understand you've fallen on some hard times.

MILLER: The mill is not milling. The churn is not churning.

DEVIL: Hard times indeed. Terrible shame. Suppose I offered to strike you a bargain that would put an end to your suffering.

MILLER: A bargain? What sort of a bargain?

DEVIL: I will shower you in riches if you but give me what stands in your backyard.

MILLER: (*Thinking aloud to himself*) What stands in my backyard? Hmm? Let's see. What stands in my backyard? Why, nothing stands in my backyard but my apple tree. Can that be all this dark, shadowy man wants from me? My apple tree in exchange for riches? Sounds too easy. Perhaps I should be cautious. (*Pause*) NAH. What the heck? Riches for an apple tree. (*To* DEVIL) You got a deal!

DEVIL: Very well. In three years' time I will come and take what is mine. (*He retreats into the darkness chortling softly yet evily to himself.*)

MILLER: Wow. What a bargain. I sure am one shrewd negotiator. My wife will be so pleased. I have ended all of our troubles and sorrow. I knew that coming to the forest to chop some wood was a good idea.

(MILLER'S WIFE *comes running onstage.*)

MILLER'S WIFE: Giuseppe. Giuseppe. My goodness. What on earth is happening? Our cupboards are overflowing with game, our trunks and boxes are filled with gold coins, our torn and ragged clothes have turned to velvet. (*She looks at her finger.*) Ahhh! Look, my ring has turned to gold. What can be the meaning of this?

MILLER: My dear and darling wife, listen to me. We are saved. As I was chopping wood I came across a dark and shadowy figure who promised me great wealth if I but gave him what stands in our backyard. Pretty good deal, huh?

MILLER'S WIFE: Oh no! Say it is not so! That dark and shadowy stranger was none other than the devil himself.

MILLER: How do you figure that? A lifetime of riches for an apple tree sounds pretty good to me.

MILLER'S WIFE: What stands in our backyard is our apple tree. Yes. But also in our backyard, sweeping with a willow broom, is...our daughter.

MILLER: No. I've been tricked.

MILLER'S WIFE: When you strike a bargain with the devil you must stay true to your word.

MILLER: And so in three years' time he will come to claim our daughter? We are cursed. What can we do?

MILLER'S WIFE: There is nothing we can do. We must go home and enjoy our last three years of happiness. We must tell our daughter of the terrible fate that awaits her.

MILLER: Oh my God. Can you ever forgive me? I knew not what I was doing.

MILLER'S WIFE: I know, Giuseppe. I know. Come on. There there. Shhh. Let's go home now. Shhh.

MILLER: It seemed like such a good idea at the time.

Scene Four

(ANN and DAVE's house. ANN is entering.)

ANN: Jesus Christ. Fucking animals. Honey? What a day. Fuck me. What time is it? There is no getting out of there. Dave? You're not going to believe the nonsense they threw at me. I have to tell you about this. Are you here? I'm sorry I'm late. Are we still going out? Honey?

(DAVE enters.)

DAVE: Hi.

ANN: Hi. Do we have time for a quick drink before we go? I need to unwind. I'm really sorry I'm so late. You have to hear about this day.

DAVE: We're not going out. I cooked.

ANN: You what?

DAVE: I made dinner here. To surprise you.

ANN: No. Oh, honey, I'm so sorry. Is it all ruined?

DAVE: Pretty much.

ANN: Did you make...?

DAVE: Of course.

ANN: Just like for our first anniversary. That is so sexy.

DAVE: We've been married for ten years.

ANN: We're too young to have been married for ten years.

DAVE: And you blew it off.

ANN: I was at work.

DAVE: How could you do that?

ANN: I'm sorry. There was nothing I could do.

DAVE: You could have called.

ANN: I was totally overwhelmed.

DAVE: Don't you care?

ANN: I didn't have a choice.

DAVE: That's it?

ANN: What do you want me to say?

DAVE: I don't know if this is working.

ANN: What?

DAVE: I'm not happy. We need to...I don't know. Do...something.

ANN: If you had gotten promoted, you'd be doing the same thing. Men do this all the time. Are you jealous?

DAVE: It's our anniversary. That means something. You could make the time.

ANN: I'm doing my best. I really am. What do you want me to do? Quit?

DAVE: No.

ANN: Because I will.

DAVE: We have a plan.

ANN: Well then? Why don't we get off the plan?

DAVE: And do what?

ANN: I don't know.

DAVE: No. The plan is a good plan. You know that. I just need you to be better. Better than you are.

ANN: What does that mean?

DAVE: I make the time for you. I take your phone calls.

ANN: I can't be in two places at the same time. I can't juggle everything perfectly. I want more too, you know.

DAVE: Like what? This is a dream come true for you.

ANN: None of this makes sense to me anymore. I'm tired of pretending to be happy instead of actually trying to be happy. Something is...missing.

DAVE: Something like what?

ANN: I don't know.

DAVE: You don't know? Well, you think about it. Think about what you want and what you're willing to do to make it happen. And when you come to some sort of a decision, schedule me into your Filofax and maybe we can talk about it.

(DAVE *exits.* ANN *sings:*)

ANN: If I want to, I can pretend that everything I wanted
is everything I need.
If I want to, I can pretend that I'm not trapped here
no indeed.

I can make believe
That I'm really happy
It's a most formidable task.

This is it. This is mine.
Everything is fine.
So why on earth do I gotta ask...

What do you do when you
get what you want? But you
want something other than that
what you got? Which is
what you wanted when you
thought you knew what you
really really wanted in the
first place.

I probably need to get out more.

(*If the song is not used,* DAVE *should exit and* ANN *should be left alone on stage for a beat, looking out.*)

Scene Five

(*In the darkness Mendelssohn's wedding march plays. The lights come up very slowly on* JULIE *in a beautiful, white wedding dress; she is looking at the ground. As the lights fade up the music starts to distort. Like an echo of a dream. As* JULIE *lifts her head we see that she is crying hysterically. Her face a ruined canvas of smeared makeup. She looks down at a wrinkled letter she is holding in her hand. She crumples it in her fist and throws it to the floor as her tears turn to screams. Lights crossfade to ERIC, who is driving on a highway dressed in a tuxedo. Night. The sound of cars.)*

ERIC: Dear Julie. I'm sorry. But my reasons for leaving are solely due to my own inadequacies and problems. I need to face up to my life, and you can't be a part of that. I thought I could make this work, but I simply can't. Perhaps it would have been easier and safer to stay, but it would have been wrong. It probably doesn't seem so to you now, but believe me—by leaving I am doing you a huge favor. Please don't try to find me. I am no longer who I was. I don't expect you to understand or forgive, but I hope that you will get on with your life and find the happiness out there you so genuinely deserve.

(Lights up dim on MAIDEN.)

ERIC: As for me, I will always remember your kindness. Your compassion. Your true inner goodness. I don't deserve a place in your heart. Please forget me. Eric.

Scene Six

(MAIDEN, dressed in white, is drawing a circle around herself with chalk in the yard. MILLER and MILLER'S WIFE enter.)

MILLER: Well, my darling wife, it has been exactly three years to the day since I made that hideous bargain. Looks like that wicked devil is not going to claim his reward after all.

MILLER'S WIFE: Oh make no mistake, the devil does not forgo what is his. He will not renege on his bargain.

MILLER: What is it our daughter is doing? Drawing on the ground like that? She looks almost as if she were in a trance.

MILLER'S WIFE: She is guided by the ages. Drawing on the wisdom of those who came before her. She is taking instruction from a faraway time.

MILLER: Mm. Right. Whatever. Anyway...

(DEVIL enters ready to party.)

DEVIL: O K you deadbeats, Big Daddy's here. Fork over the goods.

MILLER: Oh you wicked, wicked devil. Is there anything I can say to make you change your mind?

DEVIL: Uh. Not likely, but go ahead and give it a shot.

MILLER: Please. Have mercy on us. I was but a poor miller. You duped me. I did not know for what I was bargaining. I love my daughter with all my heart and soul.

DEVIL: Yeah, well, tough luck. Them's the breaks, pops. Look before you leap, know what I mean? Now hand over the broad.

MILLER: She is right over there. Take her if you must.

(DEVIL *sees the* MAIDEN. *Walks over to her. Gets propelled backwards as hard and as far as possible.*)

DEVIL: What gives, pops?

MILLER: Oh she's drawing on the wisdom of...I don't know.

DEVIL: Hmmm. I don't like the looks of this. I got a bad feeling. I think the chick's too clean. Tell you what. Here's the deal. No bathing. Three weeks. Got it.

(MAIDEN *exits.*)

DEVIL: I'll be back. I'm serious about this. No baths. Not even a little, understand? No flippity bippity with a sponge under the pits, huh. No wiggity diggitys with a little splash of water on the back, got it? O K, then. No baths. No water. No nothing. Blah-hah-hah.

(DEVIL *exits.* MILLER *and* MILLER'S WIFE *look at each other then out at the audience.* DEVIL *reenters.*)

DEVIL: O K, it's three weeks later, where the hell's the little chiquita? I'm a busy guy, you know. Don't have time for all this nonsense.

(MAIDEN *reenters. She is as dirty and animal-like as possible.*)

DEVIL: Oh yeah! That's much better. Prime goods.

(DEVIL *crosses towards* MAIDEN. *As he is getting closer* MAIDEN *begins to cry into her hands.* DEVIL *is stopped as if walking into an invisible force field.*)

DEVIL: Oh give me a break. Tears cried by a true heart are like holy water up my ass. Stop crying. Come on. Cut it out now. No more crying.

(MAIDEN *begins to stop crying.*)

DEVIL: Shit. Now with all these tears, her hands are still too clean. We gotta get rid of all the holy water. Miller. Cut off her hands.

MILLER & MILLER'S WIFE: What!?

DEVIL: You heard me. Did I stutter? Cut 'em off. Let's go, let's go, let's go, times a wastin'.

MILLER: Surely you cannot ask me to cut off the hands of my daughter.

DEVIL: I can and I will and, if I'm not mistaken, I just did. *(He picks up* MILLER's *ax.)* Here you are. Let's go. Chop chop. Do the deed.

MILLER: I cannot.

(DEVIL gets in MILLER's *face very seriously.)*

DEVIL: I am not toying with you. Do you understand me? This is not a game. You do not get to decide what you can and cannot do. You made a bargain. Now cut off that little bitch's hands or you die, your wife dies, and this whole fucking village dies.

*(*MILLER *takes the ax and walks over towards* MAIDEN.)*

MILLER: My daughter. I am so sorry. I have some bad news. I'm going to have to chop off your hands. There is nothing I can do.

MAIDEN: You will do what you must.

*(*MILLER *leads* MAIDEN *to a stump. Puts her hands on it. Raises his ax)*

MILLER: Heaven forgive me.

(He brings the ax down. A flash of blood red. A crashing thud. A brief blackout. Screams in the dark. Lights restore. MAIDEN *has bloody stumps.* MILLER *collapses to his knees.)*

DEVIL: Mine. She's mine. All mine.

(DEVIL runs towards MAIDEN. MAIDEN *begins to cry. The tears fall on her stumps. The* DEVIL *again hits an invisible force field and is stopped.)*

DEVIL: DAARRGGH. Damn it! Again with those fucking tears. Tears, tears, tears. It's three strikes and I'm out.

MILLER: Three strikes and you're out?

MILLER'S WIFE: If the Devil cannot stake his claim in three attempts, he must relinquish his prize.

DEVIL: Alright, that's it, I'm outa here. But I'll be watching you. Oh yes, make no mistake. I'll be watching. AAARRRGGHHH! *(He exits in a flurry of cacophonous madness.)*

MILLER: My God. His very words have set the woods on fire.

MILLER'S WIFE: My darling, are you alright?

MAIDEN: I am alright, Mother.

MILLER: Boy, I feel like I've aged a hundred years today. My poor daughter. Can you ever forgive me?

MAIDEN: You did what was necessary.

MILLER: Well, at least now he has no claim to you. You have no hands but we can go about rebuilding our lives. We are still very wealthy. Your mother and I can feed you and clothe you and baby you for the rest of your life.

MAIDEN: No, Father.

MILLER: What do you mean no? What more could a child ask?

MILLER'S WIFE: How 'bout for a pair of hands?

MAIDEN: This is not the proper life for me. I feel it more fitting that I should become a beggar girl. *(She launches into song:)*
A wandering beggar,
a penniless urchin.
My travels will take me
all over this land

Relying on others,
the kindness of strangers,
won't someone please
lend me a...

Sing hey nonny-nonny,
my parents were wealthy,
will all of my clothing
be tattered and torn?

The life that I led has been
suddenly dumped.
The cards I've been dealt
would suggest I've been trumped.
If you ask where I'm going
I'm bloody well stumped.

This journey I've started
will see me reborn.

(If the song is not used, simply cut it as well as the MILLER'S WIFE's next line.)

MILLER: Did you hear what she said?

MILLER'S WIFE: She has her mother's voice.

MILLER: Are you out of your mind? What is this, some sort of teenage-rebel-against-your-parents-kind of thing?

MILLER'S WIFE: She must do what she thinks is right.

MILLER: Do what she thinks is right? She should do what her father tells her to do. Sweetheart. We can live in a beautiful castle.

MAIDEN: I do not need a castle, Father.

MILLER: No, but it sure is nice.

MAIDEN: I will go a-wandering and depend on the kindness of others for sustenance.

MILLER: Depend on the kindness of others? Honey, it's a jungle out there. What do you think you're living in, some kind of fairy tale world where people are nice?

MAIDEN: ...

MILLER: Alright, alright, so you're living in a fairy tale where everyone's nice. O K. Well. If you think that's what's best...go a-wandering.

MAIDEN: Goodbye, Father. *(She kisses him on the cheek.)* Goodbye, Mother *(A hug)* I will miss you both.

(She exits. Pause. Lights up on DAVE entering.)

MILLER: Rough day.

MILLER'S WIFE: You said it.

Scene Seven

(ANN and DAVE's. DAVE is entering.)

DAVE: Ann? What a rough day. Jesus Christ. I have to tell you about this. Honey? You here? So get this, right? Remember I told you about Alex and his secretary right? Well, lately, he's been taking these two-hour, three-martini lunches, and when he comes back he's feeling a little...well, frisky, you know? So. Anyway, turns out his wife had decided to give him a little surprise today...

(DAVE sees a piece of paper on the table. He picks it up and starts to read it. Lights come up on ANN driving.)

DAVE: ...What?

Scene Eight

(A roadside diner. At lights up MOE is cleaning the counter. After a beat ERIC enters in his tuxedo and sits at the counter. Note: This scene is a bit dreamlike. Go with it.)

MOE: Mornin'. Coffee?

ERIC: Yeah.

MOE: Rough party?

ERIC: What? *(Notices his tuxedo)* Oh. This. No. *(He looks at a menu. Looks up)* I'll have...

MOE: Two eggs over easy. Side a bacon. Wheat toast and an O J?

ERIC: Yeah. Um?

MOE: Yes?

ERIC: I have a problem.

MOE: Yes?

ERIC: I don't think I have any money. I...um. I left in a bit of a hurry, and, uh, I can't really go back and...I don't have my wallet on me.

MOE: No money huh?

ERIC: I really need to eat something. Please. I'll mail you a check or something, I swear.

MOE: Hmm. Interesting.

ERIC: Or here. *(He takes off his wedding ring)* I'll trade you this ring. I'll trade you my ring for two eggs over easy.

MOE: That looks like it's worth a lot of money.

ERIC: It cost a lot of money, that doesn't mean it's worth anything.

MOE: Nah. You keep the ring. Eggs are on the house.

ERIC: Really? Oh, thank you. Thank you very much.

MOE: So, uh. A guy's gotta ask. Why the tux?

ERIC: I left my wife.

MOE: Uh-huh.

ERIC: She's not really my wife.

MOE: Uh-huh?

ERIC: I left her at the altar.

MOE: Oof.

ERIC: I deserve to die.

MOE: Why didn't you want to marry her?

ERIC: What? Oh. I couldn't.

MOE: How come? *(Pause)*

ERIC: What state am I in?

MOE: You don't know what state you're in?

ERIC: I've been driving.

MOE: What state would you like to be in?

ERIC: I'm headed for New York.

MOE: Where'd you start?

ERIC: Seattle.

MOE: You still got a ways to go. Gotta cross the Mississippi just up ahead.

ERIC: Mmm. This place called Miller's?

MOE: Yup.

ERIC: You Miller?

MOE: Moe.

ERIC: Moe Miller?

MOE: That's me. And you are...?

ERIC: I don't know.

MOE: Not even a name?

ERIC: Eric, I guess. Evan? No. I gotta stay with Eric, I think.

MOE: Pleasure.

ERIC: What?

MOE: I said it's a pleasure to meet you.

ERIC: Oh. Thanks. Same here. (Pause) Moe?

MOE: Yo.

ERIC: Am I awake?

MOE: You want to be awake?

ERIC: I want to be dead.

MOE: You're not dead.

ERIC: Moe?

MOE: Yo.

ERIC: I'm gay.

MOE: We serve gays here.

ERIC: What?

MOE: I say you can still have your eggs even though you're gay.

ERIC: Oh. Thanks.

(ANN enters. Sits at counter.)

MOE: Mornin'. Coffee?

ANN: Yes. Thank you.

(MOE gets the coffee.)

MOE: Here you go.

ANN: *(To* ERIC*)* Would you pass the milk?

ERIC: Sure.

ANN: *(To* MOE*)* How far to Seattle?

MOE: Seattle? Oh you got a ways to go yet. You still gotta cross the Mississippi up ahead.

ANN: Mmm. Thank you. *(To* ERIC*)* Rough party?

ERIC: What? *(Notices his tuxedo)* Oh. This. No. I left my wife-to-be at the altar.

ANN: You did that?

ERIC: Yes.

ANN: Just now?

ERIC: Basically.

*(*ANN *throws her cup of coffee in his face.)*

ANN: Fuck you, asshole.

ERIC: *(Completely calmly)* Ow. You know, that's scalding hot coffee. That really hurts.

ANN: You deserved it. Can I get a refill here?

*(*MOE *refills* ANN'*s coffee.)*

ERIC: I didn't just leave her for no reason, you know.

ANN: Whatever.

ERIC: I did it for her own good.

ANN: Oh I'm sure. You don't just...

ERIC: O K, so I did it for my own good too.

ANN: ...leave people.

ERIC: You don't know what it's like to live a lie. To wake up everyday and pretend to be something you're not.

ANN: I know exactly how that feels.

ERIC: I'm gay.

ANN: Congratulations.

ERIC: I say those words and I expect lightning to strike. The roof to cave in. Doesn't anyone care?

ANN: *(To* MOE*)* Can I have...?

MOE: Two eggs over easy. Side a bacon. Wheat toast and an O J?

ANN: Yeah.

MOE: Comin' up.

ERIC: Why is it that I say those two words and no one flinches. I'm a completely different person than I was yesterday. Why does nobody see that?

ANN: *(Removing the $100 bill)* Say, can you break a hundred?

MOE: *(Regarding the bill)* Hundred? "For the true winner"? Nah, you keep that. You might need it. Eggs are on the house.

ERIC: I thought if I did this the whole world would end, but this isn't so bad. I should have done this a long time ago. Hey, do you think it's possible to just disappear?

ANN: What?

ERIC: I'm hoping to disappear.

ANN: You want to disappear because you're gay?

ERIC: No, I want to reappear because I'm gay.

ANN: Well, I don't think it's possible.

ERIC: No?

ANN: You can run from your problems, but you can't just disappear. That's retarded.

ERIC: What problems are you running from?

ANN: None of your business.

ERIC: Hey, I told you I was gay.

ANN: I said, none of your fucking business.

ERIC: Sorry. Are you from New York?

ANN: Yeah. Why?

ERIC: That's where I'm headed.

ANN: Turn back now. It's a hell hole.

ERIC: I can't. I'm going to see someone from my past, and if I don't find him I'll...well, I don't know what I'll do. I have to reappear, so I'm still going to disappear, even if you think it's retarded.

ANN: I'm sorry, I didn't mean to be rude.

ERIC: That's O K.

ANN: Sorry about the coffee. I'm just in a bit of a state right now.

ERIC: What happenned?

ANN: I don't know. I...I guess I've been trying so hard to pretend that everything's O K, that it just all came crashing down.

ERIC: Yeah?

ANN: I mean, I'm standing there in Starbucks, right? Reading some article about Bill Gates's house.

ERIC: Oh, brother.

ANN: I know, it sounds stupid, but it suddenly seems like the most incredible place I can possibly imagine. Do you know anything about it?

ERIC: Bits and pieces.

ANN: The house knows what kind of music you like, and it plays it for you wherever you are. The paintings on the wall change to match your taste. The air is always the perfect temperature for your body.

ERIC: Wow.

ANN: It's like some sort of fairy tale castle where the entire house responds to your every desire. I can't imagine that. I have to see it. Touch it.

ERIC: So you just picked up and left?

ANN: I looked down at my coffee, and I looked down at the picture of the house, and the next thing I know I'm in a car headed west.

ERIC: How are you going to get in?

ANN: I don't know.

ERIC: But you had to go.

ANN: I have a great job, and they'll probably fire me. I have a husband whom I love, and I just...abandoned him. But...I just had to...do it anyway. It would have been easier to stay and remain asleep, but I suddenly felt that if I stayed I would die.

MOE: Here are your breakfasts. (*He puts the plates down.*)

(MAIDEN *enters. Her stumps are bound in gauze. The effect of her entrance on* ERIC *and* ANN *is a bit like if Bugs Bunny walked in.*)

MAIDEN: Excuse me, kind people, can anyone assist me? The wind and the road are my new parents. I have no ducats nor gold coins, and I'm a-wandering in search of a new life.

(ERIC *and* ANN *look at each other.*)

(*Blackout*)

END OF ACT ONE

ACT TWO

Scene Nine

(A chamber of the KING's. KING and GARDENER are talking.)

KING: Tell me this again.

GARDENER: I swear, my Lord, it is the truth.

KING: This maiden had no hands?

GARDENER: None, my Lord.

KING: And she was in my orchard?

GARDENER: That is right, my Lord.

KING: And how did she get into my orchard? How did she pass over the moat?

GARDENER: A spirit.

KING: A spirit. Hmm. How interesting. Hold on one second. *(Speaks into an intercom)* Candy...?? *(Voice: "Yes, Mr King?")* Get Merle in here pronto will ya?

(MERLE enters. He is dressed as a stereotypical wizard.)

KING: Merle, good to see you.

MERLE: Pardon my appeerence, I was just boiling eye of newt. A messy affair. How can I be of assistance, my Lord?

KING: One of my peaches is missing. Now then, tell Merle what you just told me.

GARDENER: I was in the King's orchard, numbering all the peaches as is the wish of my Lord, when I swear that I did see a handless maiden guided by a spirit in white. The spirit did cause the waters of the moat to part, allowing this handless maiden access to the orchard. The maiden tried to bite a peach but the branch was too high. Next thing I knew, the very branch did bend down to meet the handless maiden's lips. She bit of the peach, and then they were gone.

KING: Sounds like a load a hooey to me. What do you say, Merle?

MERLE: What he says is possible, my Lord.

KING: Come now, I think our friend the gardener here got a little hungry, stole a peach, and is now trying to cover up with some fantastical story about handless maidens and spirits in white.

MERLE: That is also possible, my Lord. But what he says does have a ring of truth to mine ear. I suggest that twenty-four hours after the initial sighting we make our way back to the same spot and see if the handless maiden and her spirit guide do come again.

KING: What time did you see them?

GARDENER: (Looking at his watch) Doa! We have but five minutes.

KING: Let's go.

(KING, GARDENER, and MERLE cross to another side of the stage. They look offstage. There is a peachtree branch visible.)

KING: So, is this the spot?

GARDENER: This is it, my Lord.

KING: Well. I don't see anything. You want to amend your story right about now?

MERLE: Look. Off in yonder distance. (He points offstage.)

GARDENER: It. It is she. It. It is her. It. It is them.

KING: Well, well, well. Will you lookey here? It is exactly as you say. I was wrong to have doubted you, my faithful gardener. Look. The spirit in white is parting the moat.

GARDENER: They are crossing.

MERLE: They're coming this way.

(MAIDEN enters and stands beneath the peachtree branch, which magically bends down to meet the MAIDEN. She bites the peach.)

KING: My God. She is the most beautiful woman I've ever seen.

GARDENER: Yeah...if you go for chicks with no hands.

KING: Silence. I must speak to her.

MERLE: Careful, my Lord. We do not know if she is of this world.

KING: Well, how do we find out?

MERLE: Allow me to approach her. (He walks over towards MAIDEN.) Do not be afraid, gentle creature, I mean you no harm. Tell me, fair maiden: Are you of this world or not of this world?

MAIDEN: I am of *the* world yet not of *this* world.

MERLE: Hmm, interesting *(He crosses back towards* KING *and* GARDENER, *talking to himself.)* A riddle. Once of *the* world, yet not of *this* world. Once of *the* world, yet not of *this* world.... I have no idea what that means.

KING: Well. Is she human or spirit?

MERLE: She is...both!?

KING: I am enthralled. *(He crosses to* MAIDEN.*)* I shall not foresake you. I will replace your missing hands with hands of silver. From this day forward I shall care for you. Will you be my bride?

*(*MAIDEN *looks out to the audience.)*

Scene Ten

*(*PETER *and* LISA *at a bar.* PETER *is dressed as a* KING, LISA *as a Princess* [MAIDEN]. *Perhaps the other bar from Scene Eleven is visible with* BARTENDER *behind it and* MAX *drinking at it. Perhaps not.)*

PETER: So the magician says to the gardener, "Don't worry, it all went right up my sleeve."

LISA: Oh, brother.

PETER: You don't think that's funny?

LISA: Who told you that one?

PETER: Because he was...

LISA: I get it. Believe me. I get it. Let me guess—

LISA & PETER: Chris.

LISA: What time is it?

PETER: Ten-ten.

LISA: You want to head over?

PETER: We'll be early.

LISA: I thought the party started at nine. *(Pause)* Do we have to stay long?

PETER: We're in—we're out. Soon as I finish my drink, we're off like a prom dress.

LISA: You always say that.

PETER: "Off like a prom dress?"

LISA: No, "we're in—we're out" and then we end up staying forever.

PETER: We won't stay forever, I promise.

LISA: Whatever.

PETER: "Don't worry, it all went right up my sleeve."? You really don't think that's funny?

LISA: Do you mean, should you tell it at the party?

PETER: Yeah.

LISA: No.

PETER: O K.

LISA: This is definitely a costume party, right?

PETER: It's Halloween.

LISA: That doesn't mean it's a costume party.

PETER: It's a costume party.

LISA: I walk in there looking like Snow White and everyone else is in jeans, you're a dead man.

PETER: Relax. We go. We say hello. I kiss Steven's ass. We leave.

LISA: Oh, speaking of ass-kissing, do you think my pecan pie is enough to bring to Thanksgiving?

PETER: Sure.

LISA: Your father's not allergic to pecans, is he?

PETER: No.

LISA: Why do you think he doesn't like me?

PETER: Who?

LISA: Your father.

PETER: He doesn't like anybody.

LISA: He liked your other girlfriends, right?

PETER: More or less.

LISA: So then?

PETER: I don't know, Lisa. I've been trying for thirty years to get him to like me. You want to know why he doesn't like you, ask him.

LISA: Sorry.

(ERIC enters the bar dressed in his tuxedo, looking around.)

PETER: Now who's this guy supposed to be? Jimmy Stewart in "It's A Wonderful Life"?

(PETER and ERIC see each other. ERIC comes over.)

PETER: Oh my. Well, well, well. Will you lookey here.

ERIC: Hi.

PETER: Eric. This is my fiancée, Lisa. Lisa this is Eric. A friend of mine from...way back.

ERIC: Hi.

LISA: Hi.

PETER: Gosh, Eric, how long has it been?

ERIC: It's been a while.

PETER: Yes it has. We were actually just on our way out.

ERIC: I understand.

LISA: Halloween party.

ERIC: Yes. You look like a king with his queen.

PETER: Thank you. You look like shit.

LISA: Peter. Rough party?

ERIC: I've been driving.

LISA: Are you alright?

ERIC: Oh, sure. Fine.

LISA: Are you meeting someone here? Do you want to join us?

PETER: Somehow I don't think joining us is quite what he had in mind.

ERIC: No. You know, it's not actually a coincidence that I find you here.

PETER: No?

ERIC: I've been looking for you. It's fairly important, actually. Something personal I need to talk to you about. I'm in a bit of a bind. With um...something you can help me with. If...I could...

PETER: Unfortunately, we really are in a bit of a hurry.

LISA: Don't be rude. He needs to talk to you.

PETER: I'll tell you what, here's my card. Why don't you call me tomorrow and we'll see if we can't straighten things out.

ERIC: I understand.

PETER: (To LISA) Come on, we should get going.

LISA: Well, it was nice meeting you.

ERIC: Same here. I'll call you tomorrow.

PETER: You do that.

(PETER *and* LISA *exit.*)

LISA: *(As exiting)* How do you know that guy?

ERIC: Oh boy. Am I fucked.

(ERIC *"swipes" past the bar and as he does it transforms through lights, sound, practicals, acting postures, and/or set pieces into a different bar.*)

Scene Eleven

(MAX *at a bar talking to* BARTENDER.)

MAX: So the magician says to the Gardener, "Don't worry, it all went right up my sleeve."

(BARTENDER *laughs.*)

MAX: Give me another one.

BARTENDER: Why don't you slow down? Drinkin' ain't gonna solve your problems.

MAX: Oh, hmm. I'm sorry. I ask you? I don't remember.

BARTENDER: I'm just trying to look out for you, my friend.

MAX: I know. I'm sorry.

BARTENDER: You're gonna have to pick yourself back up. You can't go on like this forever. Listen. I seen this woman in here last night. Asking everyone in the place if they work for Microsoft. Said she'd be back tonight. Maybe you could, uh...you know, give her some inside dope.

MAX: Yeah, maybe.

BARTENDER: Wait 'til you see her. Who knows? Maybe it'll be love at first sight.

(ANN *enters.*)

BARTENDER: Burger with fries. Speak of the devil.

(*It is indeed love at first sight.* ANN *sits at the bar. Removes the $100 bill*)

BARTENDER: What can I get for you?

ANN: Gin and tonic.

BARTENDER: I'm out of gin.

ANN: You're out of gin? You're a bar. You can't be out of gin.

BARTENDER: Getcha something else?

MAX: Give her a fuzzy navel.

ANN: No. I don't drink drinks with cute little names. Vodka tonic.

MAX: Give her a fuzzy navel. It's on me.

BARTENDER: Peach Schnapps I got.

MAX: You'll like it.

BARTENDER: Comin' up.

ANN: Thank you. *(To the $100 bill)* Can't seem to get rid of you. *(She puts the $100 bill away.)*

MAX: So what brings you around these parts?

ANN: You work for Microsoft?

MAX: Everyone works for Microsoft somehow. If they don't yet, they will.

ANN: You don't look like a computer geek.

MAX: Computer geek? I don't even have a T V.

ANN: So what do you do?

MAX: I build furniture.

ANN: For Microsoft?

MAX: For the big cheese. For his house. Redwoods are my specialty. He loves the Redwoods.

ANN: Can you get me in there?

MAX: Everyone wants to see the big house. Want to know the truth?

ANN: Yeah.

MAX: It's just a fuckin' house. It's pretty gross if you ask me.

ANN: I don't care. I still need to see it.

MAX: And why should I get you in?

ANN: I left my entire life behind to see this house.

MAX: Gee, that makes sense.

ANN: It doesn't make any sense, but I still have to do it.

MAX: What are you, some kind of freak?

ANN: No, I'm really charming once you get to know me.

MAX: Yeah?

BARTENDER: Here ya go. *(He exits.)*

MAX: What's your name?

ANN: Ann. *(She sips the drink.)*

MAX: I'm Max.

ANN: Nice name.

MAX: Thank you. You married?

ANN: Oh, and here I thought you were just buying me a drink.

MAX: It's a simple question.

ANN: Not always. You married?

MAX: No. No, I'm not married. Was.

ANN: Things didn't work out?

MAX: Huh. No. No, they didn't.

ANN: What happenned?

MAX: I don't really want to talk about it....

ANN: Oh, come on...

MAX: ...tell me about you.

ANN: ...you buy a girl a drink, the least you can do is tell her your life story. It's what all the other boys do.

MAX: Oh, is that how it works?

ANN: Those are the rules. If you wanna play, play fair.

MAX: Well, she...died.

ANN: Oh. I'm sorry. How did she die?

MAX: You don't give up, do you?

ANN: I saw this movie once where the way the cops nailed the killer was because he was the only one who *didn't* ask how the victim had died. So you have to tell or I'll think you think I killed her.

MAX: What?

ANN: Here, look, bartender, give him another one.

MAX: Uh, I think I've had enough.

ANN: Nope. You buy me one. I buy you one. I'll tell you about Dave, if you tell me about...

MAX: Sharon.

ANN: See how easy it is.

MAX: Look...

ANN: Come on, what have you got to lose? Just talk to me. If it doesn't go well, you never have to see me again. But, if it does go well...you show me the house.

MAX: O K. Fine. I was uh...out of state. Doing a fair. That's what I did before I started working for the big cheese. And uh...some guy broke into our house and uh...killed...her. Killed her then...raped her.

(ANN *starts to laugh.*)

MAX: What the hell's so funny?

ANN: *(Still laughing)* It's not, it's not funny. God, that's awful.

MAX: Ha ha ha. Maybe this isn't such a good idea. (MAX *starts to go.*)

ANN: No, wait. Please don't go. I'm sorry. I didn't know. I was just shocked I didn't mean any offense, and...here, the drinks are on me. *(She puts the $100 bill on the bar.)*

MAX: I haven't even said her name out loud in a year and you think it's funny?

ANN: Not funny. Ridiculous. Absurd. How can you make sense of something like that? But if you can't laugh...I don't know.

MAX: It hurts.

ANN: I know. But it's not like "not talking about it" is gonna make it go away.

MAX: No.

ANN: You know, when I started driving out here I thought I must be out of my mind. Throwing everything away on what seemed like a whim. But I think it's actually a lot worse to stay trapped in what you know. Sometimes you just need to take a chance.

MAX: Would you throw that drink in my face if I told you you were beautiful?

ANN: No.

MAX: You're very beautiful.

ANN: You're very beautiful too. You, uh, chat up all the girls in this place?

MAX: No. I don't know how to talk to girls. I married her when I was nineteen.

ANN: Who?

MAX: My wife.

ANN: Who?

MAX: ...Sharon.

ANN: You do O K.

MAX: Thanks. You like that fuzzy navel?

ANN: Peachey. Sweet.

MAX: Yeah.

ANN: Max?

MAX: Yeah?

ANN: Do you really build furniture for that house?

MAX: Nope.

ANN: I didn't think so.

MAX: Sorry. You want to keep talking to me?

ANN: Of course.

MAX: Ann?

ANN: Yeah?

MAX: I really build furniture for that house.

(As the lights change, MAX and ANN exit. MESSENGER enters.)

Scene Twelve

(A MESSENGER running in the forest.)

MESSENGER: I hate this fuckin' war. This fucking war. Gimme that land. Gimme those ducats. *(She picks up the $100 bill.)* Fight fight fight fight fight. *(She pockets the bill.)* King's needed on the battlefield. Queen's at home with his mother. And I gotta run around like a jerk, delivering messages back and forth, back and forth, always bloody back and forth. I'm just trying not to get killed. Aw, geez. My friggin' feet are killing me. I wonder if I could just lay me down by the side of this here brook. Just for a minute. You know—rest the old weary eyes. *(She lays down. Closes eyes. After a beat bolts upright)* I am not going to sleep, though. Nuh-uh. Too much important work to do. *(She goes to sleep.)*

(From out of the darkness steps the DEVIL.)

DEVIL: Well well well. Let's just see what we have here. *(He takes the message and reads it.)* Dear King. Your beautiful wife has given birth to a beautiful baby boy. Glorious news. Love, Mother. Nyah-Nyah-Nyah. Foo! So... The Handless Bitch has mothered a child. Well. We'll just see about that. *(He takes out a pen and scrawls on the message.)* New new new, hoo hoo hoo, hubba hubba doo doo. Love, Mother. *(He replaces message and exits.)* Wake up!

MESSENGER: *(Awakening)* Wha-? Who? Not sleeping. Oh, sheesh. O K.
I feel better. Now then. Gotta get this message to the King.

(MESSENGER *starts walking. Meets up with the* KING.)

MESSENGER: Hello, my Lord. I come bearing news from the castle.

KING: News from the castle? Oh, goodey-goodey. Is it about my wife?
I cannot wait to see.

(MESSENGER *hands* KING *the message, which* KING *reads aloud.*)

KING: Dear King. You wife has given birth to a child which is half dog.
Seems that in your absence she has been copulating with the beasts in the
woods. Please advise. Love, Mother. Oh my. Well, this is terrible news.
What am I to do? Can this really be so? My wife? Think think think think
think. Messenger. Send back the following message. *(He scrawls a message
and hands the new message to the* MESSENGER.*)* Be sure you do not dally.
Move with great haste. Over hill and valley. There is no time to waste.

MESSENGER: No my Lord!

(KING *exits.* MESSENGER *heads back towards the castle.*)

MESSENGER: "Yes, my Lord; no, my Lord. Do this. Do that. Hurry up." Fuck
you! As soon as I save enough gold coins, I'm blowin' this dead-end job.

(DEVIL *sticks his head out of the shadows.* MESSENGER *lets out a big yawn.*)

MESSENGER: Aw, gee, I'm suddenly feeling very sleepy again. I could swear
I just rested mine eyes. *(Another yawn. Sits)* Maybe I'll just sit down for a
second and, you know...just for a second. *(She falls asleep.)*

(DEVIL *approaches and reads the message.*)

DEVIL: Well, well, well. Let's just see what little Kingy has to say about his
predicament. *(Reading)* Dear Mother. Can your news be true? Please send
confirmation. Love, King. Oh, no, no, no. This will not do at all. Please
allow me. *(He scrawls on the message.)* Hubbidy-hubbidy-hubbidy-hubbidy
wicka-wacka-woo. There, that's much better. *(He returns the message to the*
MESSENGER *and exits.)* Wake up.

MESSENGER: Oh boy. I feel much better. Alright now. On with my journey.
Back to the castle.

(MESSENGER *continues on. Runs into the* KING'S MOTHER—CRONEY.)

CRONEY: Messenger, you've returned at last. What the devil took you so
long?

MESSENGER: Not sleeping. No! Not me. No way. No, ma'am. Nuh-uh.
No sleeping for me.

CRONEY: Did the King send back a reply?

MESSENGER: You bet your britches he did. *(Hands* CRONEY *the message)*

CRONEY: *(Reading)* Mother. Kill the child and the woman. Immediately. Love, King. P S: Please be sure to cut out and keep the woman's eyes and tongue for confirmation. *(Pause)* Heavens to Murgatroy. What am I to do? I must consult...my book. *(She exits.)*

MESSENGER: Oh no, no, no. Not again. She's gonna send me out there again, I know it. I just know it. Oh, this is ridiculous. Can't we be done with this? I mean, did I mention that there's a fuckin' WAR going on out there? That's dangerous. Geez. Why can't things be easy like they are in the real world?

Scene Thirteen

*(*ERIC *outside* PETER'*s.* ERIC *enters, looking at a business card. He goes to ring a doorbell. Stops. Straightens up. Closes his eyes.* PETER *enters from behind him. Note: This scene is a fantasy, feel free to go over the top.)*

PETER: Hello.

ERIC: Hi.

PETER: That was quite a little scare you gave me.

ERIC: I know, I'm sorry. But I had to talk to you.

PETER: So. Talk.

ERIC: I want to come back.

PETER: Really?

ERIC: I've been so miserable without you. The times we had together, I mean...it's what makes life worth living, don't you think?

PETER: Go on.

ERIC: I miss you so desperately. I threw everything away to come back to you.

PETER: Well, I must say, this is very touching. Who wouldn't want the lover who spurned him to come crawling back on his knees.

ERIC: Consider me begging then. *(He breaks into song:)*
I have nothing
Not a dollar
Just a car
And a tux
And a credit card
For gasoline
Which sort of counts as a couple of bucks
And I want to be

The me I am
Whenever I'm with you
I'm sorry
I'm so sorry
For what I put you through
Everybody else's life is normal
Everybody seems to have a clue
And I want to be
The me I am
Whenever I'm with you.

(If the song is not used, cut it, and replace with the next line for ERIC:*)*

ERIC: I have nothing. Not a dollar. Just a car and a tux. I want to be me again. The me I am when I'm with you.

PETER: Things certainly haven't been the same for me since you left.

ERIC: They haven't? Me neither. I don't care how much time has passed, this is the only life I want.

PETER: What happened to what's her name?

ERIC: Julie. I left her.

PETER: I wish I had the courage to leave Lisa.

ERIC: You do. We can start over. I made a mistake, but I'm back.

PETER: I wouldn't even know where to start.

ERIC: One step at a time.

PETER: You make it sound like a twelve-step program.

ERIC: It is what it is. Just start with a kiss.

PETER: Just a kiss?

ERIC: That's where we start. We'll see where it goes from there.

PETER: Alright.

*(*ERIC *approaches* PETER *cautiously. They kiss. Passionately.)*

PETER: I am so fucking in love with you.

*(*PETER *freezes as* ERIC *addresses the audience.)*

ERIC: Oh, God, let's hope.

(He walks around the still-frozen PETER *and rings a doorbell.)*

Scene Fourteen

(ANN *and* MAX *at* MAX's. *They are a couple.*)

MAX: So...what did you think of the house?

ANN: I still don't understand why it took three weeks before I could see it.

MAX: Security clearances. It's not easy to get in there, you know.

ANN: Uh-huh.

MAX: And, besides, I needed a carrot at the end of the stick.

ANN: Oh, I think you're enough of a carrot.

(*They kiss.*)

MAX: So. Answer the question. What did you think of the house?

ANN: Want to know the truth?

MAX: Yeah.

ANN: It's just a fuckin' house. It's pretty gross, if you ask me.

MAX: Told you.

ANN: It was just so disappointing. I mean, there I am. The temperature is perfect. I'm staring at...a Georgia O'Keefe, listening to...Aretha Franklin, everything's perfect, and I still feel like shit. I still feel like there's a hole in my life. I don't know what I thought it would give me.

MAX: A house like that can't give you anything. A perfect house is one you build with your own hands. And you know what the secret ingredient is?

ANN: What?

MAX: Love.

ANN: Build your own house?

MAX: Build you a house. For us. I have some land that I had been thinking I was going to build on. But...after Sharon died I just sort of...stopped. But now I think it's time to start building again.

ANN: Really? Don't you think...

MAX: I mean, I don't want to move too fast, and it would take some time anyway, but I think I can do it. Me and Ted together, we can make just about anything.

ANN: Oh, my god, that is about the sexiest thing I've ever heard. I love that.

MAX: Are you sure?

ANN: Build a home? For me. For us. Build a future.

MAX: That's the idea.

ANN: I came out here looking for a fantasy castle and now I get Prince Charming to go with it?

MAX: I'll do my best.

ANN: What would I do out here if I stayed?

MAX: We have lawyers in Seattle too, you know.

ANN: But maybe I don't want to be a lawyer anymore.

MAX: Then be whatever you want.

ANN: Hmm, so let's say I wanted to be a potter.

MAX: That would be great.

ANN: A chef.

MAX: I love to eat.

ANN: A gardener.

MAX: The choice is yours. (*The phone rings. Again*)

ANN: Do you want to get that?

MAX: No. I want to take you upstairs...and lay you down on the bed I built...and, even if only for an hour or so, do all we can to forget everything we ever knew.

ANN: O K. You go upstairs. I'll be up in a minute.

MAX: You O K?

ANN: I just want to be alone in a world of possibilities for a second.

(MAX *exits.* ANN *closes her eyes. The phone is still ringing. She opens her eyes.*)

ANN: What am I doing?

(*An answering machine beep...*)

Scene Fifteen

(*Three separate areas.* DAVE, JULIE, MILLER. *Lights up on* DAVE. *A "/" indicates where an overlap begins.*)

DAVE: Hello? I'm sorry, "Max", for taking up space on your machine, but I'm trying to reach my wife. Ann, I was hoping to get you, but what the hell?

(*Lights come up on* JULIE *reading a letter on pink stationery.*)

JULIE: My dearest Eric. You certainly did a great job. The gifts from Williams Sonoma made for fabulous returns, my great Uncle Phil kept saying, "buck up, it just means more alcohol for the rest of us", and the video of me crying is particularly moving.

(*Lights come up on* MILLER *reading a letter.*)

MILLER: Dear my darling daughter Maiden. Why don't you ever write to your mother and me? We sit around and wonder if we will ever hear from you again. / You're probably...

DAVE: You're probably out, I don't know, doing whatever people do for fun out there. But /I have to tell....

JULIE: I have to tell you I was devastated. I felt like a nothing and a nobody. Watching you ride off into the sunset while I am left cleaning up your mess. / I still feel...

MILLER: I still feel pretty guilty about what happened. I mean, even though I was tricked by the Devil himself, I still feel bad. / I want...

DAVE: I want you to come home to me, Ann (this is so weird, talking into a tape). I love you and...and I miss you, and...I don't know what the hell else am I supposed to say. You're everything to me, you know. / I mean...

MILLER: I mean between you, me, and the candlestick, things between your mother and me are not as good as they used to be, and believe it or not I even miss the mill. I miss milling. It was a lot of hard work, but I was happy. / Because of this...

JULIE: Because of this, my depression has led my work to suffer tremendously. I couldn't sleep or concentrate. Eric, I knew you were gay. Or wanted to be gay. I just wanted us to be happy together. But if not I will find a way to be happy without you as I hope you are without me. / I think...

DAVE: / I think...

MILLER: I think all the time about what it would be like if you were still here. I think it would be a lot better. All I have to console myself with is more money than I could have ever possibly imagined. And I mean, O K, that's not so bad. But I would trade everything to have you back. / If I cannot...

JULIE: If I cannot forget you, I can at least move forward without you. No matter what, there's a comfort in knowing that we are always moving forward towards something.

DAVE: But we can work things out, I know we can. I'm nothing without you. I'm... Please. I'm so fucking miserable. The apartment just feels so empty. I know it's hard for me to bend but I need you. You're my partner. In everything. You...you make me... You... Oh, God. I mean, I'm pretty fine actually. I mean, I'm O K. You know. No one needs to know what's inside. Just...keep...

(An answering machine beep.)

DAVE: Hello? Hello? No.

(Lights out on DAVE, who exits.)

JULIE: I've done all I can to try to find you, but apparently you cover your tracks very well. And so I send these thoughts out into the ether in the hopes they'll reach you. Sleep well, my forsaken prince. Live in peace. Love, Julie.

(She looks over the letter and then rips it in half and in half again. She exits. As she does the MESSENGER enters and picks up the pieces of her letter while on route to the MILLER.)

MILLER: Anyway. I wonder about you. I wonder if you are happy. I sure do hope that you are. Love, your father, Giuseppe.

(MILLER hands his letter to MESSENGER.)

MESSENGER: There's no address on this letter.

MILLER: I know. Just tell me you'll deliver it.

MESSENGER: I'll deliver it.

Scene Sixteen

(ERIC and PETER at PETER's).

PETER: So, you're telling me you threw everything away just to find me.

ERIC: Yes.

PETER: Where have you been sleeping?

ERIC: My car. I haven't eaten much. I...forgot my wallet.

PETER: Well, I must say, this is very touching.

ERIC: I have nothing. Not a dollar. Just a credit card for gas to get me here. I'm here. Without you I have literally nothing. A car and a tux.

PETER: I'm not sure that was your most prudent move.

ERIC: Let me back in. I'm sorry. Please. I'm... I've been in Seattle living out some bizarre version of normalcy that I can't stand. I want to be me again. The me I am when I'm with you. We're so good together but... I couldn't see that.

PETER: No, you couldn't.

ERIC: I thought our relationship was some glorious game I was allowed to play until I had to go back to real life. But this is the only real life I want.

PETER: Look. Stop, O K? I thought having you crawl back to me on your knees would feel good, but I don't want to hear this anymore. I'm happy, alright? Happy with Lisa. Happy with the way things are. The best thing you can do is leave.

ERIC: Are you happy? Or are you pretending to be happy? Because I pretended for a long time. It's easy to convince yourself.

PETER: I think you put it real well. It was a nice game we had. But at this point, and I'm sorry if this hurts you, but you're just not worth what I'd have to go through to be with you.

ERIC: None of that matters. Throw all that extraneous crap out.

PETER: Oh, like you did. Mister big responsible man, just walking away from his problems. Twice.

ERIC: Tell me, what's so great about Lisa?

PETER: None of your business.

ERIC: That's compelling. One thing. Just tell me one thing you love about her.

PETER: She...loves my jokes and I love to make her laugh. That's two.

ERIC: Fine. And now one thing about me.

PETER: You left me.

ERIC: One good thing that you love.

PETER: Loved.

ERIC: Love.

PETER: It's too late.

ERIC: Say it. Say what you used to say. Say it and I'll leave.

PETER: ...I love your eyes.

ERIC: Come on. Say it.

PETER: I love the way your whole being is transparent in your eyes.

ERIC: Go on.

PETER: I always know what you're feeling.

ERIC: And what am I feeling right now? Look in my eyes and tell me.

(They stare into each other's eyes.)

PETER: I love Lisa. And I'm going to marry Lisa. Look, I'm sorry that you threw away your life for some entitlement fantasy that you could waltz in here and win me back, but you're too late.

ERIC: Kiss me.

PETER: No.

ERIC: Give me one kiss and try to tell me there's no magic left between us.

PETER: I'm not interested anymore.

ERIC: One kiss. Come on. I came all this way. One kiss and I'll go.

PETER: Fine.

(PETER *goes to kiss* ERIC. ERIC *grabs hold. There is magic. At length* PETER *stops.*)

PETER: Now get the fuck out of my life.

Scene Seventeen

(CRONEY *and* MAIDEN *in the castle.* MAIDEN's *hands are silver. She holds the baby.*)

MAIDEN: I cannot believe the King would wish to have me killed.

CRONEY: It does seem most strange and yet his instructions are as clear as day. He even confirmed them.

MAIDEN: I don't understand. Before he went to war he was so wonderful. Giving me these hands of silver. Making me the Queen. Fathering my child. Can war have turned him into so vile a monster?

CRONEY: I don't know.

MAIDEN: What are we to do?

CRONEY: Well, certainly I will not have you killed. I have a plan. I have sacrificed a doe and saved the eyes and tongue as proof of your death. That should satisfy the King.

MAIDEN: And what am I to do?

CRONEY: You, I'm afraid, must a-wander.

MAIDEN: Again?

CRONEY: The king must not find you alive.

MAIDEN: But how am I to wander without my spirit guide?

CRONEY: Your spirit guide will be with you. She is inside you now. Do not be afraid.

MAIDEN: But I will miss you so. And the King.

CRONEY: I know, my sweet maiden. I shall miss you too. But there is no other way. Now take the baby and be gone. *(They hug.)*

MAIDEN: Alright. You know best. If you think it is right, I will do it. Goodbye.

CRONEY: Goodbye, fair maiden.

MAIDEN: Thank you for all of your kindness.

CRONEY: No problem.

MAIDEN: Think of me.

CRONEY: Go now.

(MAIDEN exits.)

CRONEY: Well. What is there to do but wait for the war to end and the King to return?

(KING enters.)

KING: Well, the war is over and I'm back. Hello, Mother. Where is my lovely wife?

CRONEY: As you commanded I have had her killed.

KING: What!?

CRONEY: She and the baby. Look. Here are the eyes and tongue as proof.

KING: Oh my God, that's disgusting! This is awful.

CRONEY: But it is just as you wished.

KING: What are you talking about?

CRONEY: Your letter.

KING: My letter said to care for my wife and the baby despite the fact that the baby is half dog.

CRONEY: Half dog. What are you talking about?

KING: That's what it said in your letter.

CRONEY: Oh no. Oh no. Something has gone terribly wrong. Your son is not half dog. It is the Devil's work. He has switched our letters to each other with these wicked and horrible lies.

KING: And to grave consequences. Now my wife and son are killed.

CRONEY: No, my Lord. I did not actually have them killed.

KING: What are you saying now?

CRONEY: I faked their deaths. These eyes and tongue are of a sacrificial doe. I could not bear to see them killed.

KING: Oh, joy! This is wonderful. Mother, you are ever so clever. So then, where are my wife and son?

CRONEY: I thought you wanted them killed so I dared not have them here upon your arrival. They have gone a-wandering.

KING: Well, where have they gone a-wandering to?

CRONEY: I do not know. They are gone for good.

KING: Oh, no, they're not. I will find them. I will search as long as the sky is blue. *(He breaks into song:)*

KING: Though the sky may burn with lightning
And the Devil's had his say
I swear on my crown
I won't let them down
Look out, I'm on my way.

They've gone I know not where
It's far too much to bear
I feel the need to share
So beware!

Though the odds are stacked against me
In the end I'll win the day
You see, here's the thing
I'm the Goddamned King!
Look out, I'm on my way!

(If the song is not used, replace the KING's prior line with the following one:)

KING: Oh, no, they're not. I will find them. I will search long and hard. I will go without food and drink. I will search as long as the sky is blue. I don't care how long it takes. I will find my wife and son.

Scene Eighteen

(MAX's)

MAX: Halloooo? I'm getting tired of waiting up here by myself. *(He enters in boxers.)* I'm starting to get hungry. We just might have to break out the chocolate sauce. Are you hiding? Are we playing a little game of hide and seek? O K. I'm coming after you. And when I find you, you're mine, all mine. You can't hide forever. I'm going to catch you. Come out, come out wherever you are. *(He finds a piece of paper. He reads it.)*

(Lights up on ANN *driving.)*

MAX: Oh, no, you don't.

Scene Nineteen

*(*MOE's *roadside diner.* MOE *is cleaning the counter. Enter* MAIDEN *with her silver hands.)*

MOE: Mornin'. Coffee?

MAIDEN: Coffee? What is coffee?

MOE: Skip it. What can I do you for?

MAIDEN: Well, kind sir, I have been wandering long and far. I need a place to cure my weariness, and I wonder if you might be the proprietor of Moe and Flo's bed and breakfast.

MOE: That's me. Moe Miller. Proprietor of Moe and Flo's. Rooms are right upstairs. If you're interested, the wife'll be happy to accommodate you.

MAIDEN: Thank you, kind sir. You are most kind indeed.

MOE: Say there, uh, just one question: Aren't you the Queen?

MAIDEN: Why, I am the Queen, indeed. How would a man such as yourself know that?

MOE: Oh, I keep up on those things. Anyway, stay as long as you like. Entrance is right around back.

MAIDEN: Thank you. You are so very kind. *(She exits.)*

(After a beat ERIC *enters.)*

MOE: Mornin'. Coffee?

ERIC: Thank you.

MOE: Say. You look awfully familiar to me.

ERIC: I came in here once a while ago.

MOE: Yeah. I knew it. I never forget a face. You were gonna give me that nice ring, right?

ERIC: That was me.

MOE: So, let me see. You were gay. That right? Looking for your boyfriend or something.

ERIC: I found him.

MOE: Congratulations.

ERIC: Turns out he has no interest in me.

MOE: Ouch. So what are you gonna do?

ERIC: I don't know. I can't go forwards and I can't go back. I need to clear my head, you know?

MOE: Time seems to have a very magical effect for that sort of thing.

ERIC: I need a place to focus. Collect my thoughts.

MOE: Well, listen, if I'm not buttin' in too much, I know the perfect place for you.

ERIC: Where?

MOE: Moe and Flo Miller's Bed & Breakfast. Right upstairs. Perfect place to clear your head.

ERIC: Really? What's so special about it?

MOE: Well. That's kinda hard to put into words. Let's just say that fairy tales can come true. It can happen to you. If...

(ANN *enters.*)

MOE: Oh. Mornin'. Coffee?

ANN: Yes, please. (*She notices* ERIC.) Hey, don't I know you from somewhere?

ERIC: You do look familiar. But I don't...

ANN: I threw coffee in your face.

ERIC: Oh yeah. Hey. How you doing? You were running away as I remember.

ANN: Yup. That was me. Still am, I guess.

ERIC: Good thing I'm not the one looking for you, huh? What are you running away from again?

ANN: Well, I was running to Seattle and now I'm running from Seattle.

ERIC: That sounds like a lot of running.

MOE: Still running huh? Still trying to find something "out there".

ANN: Yeah. I guess. What about you? I thought you were going to disappear...reappear?

ERIC: Well, I was heading to New York to find my old boyfriend, but...

ANN: Oh, right, you're gay. That was like a big deal to you as I recall.

ERIC: Right, right. I finally make the big decision to be true to myself, but I couldn't get Peter to do the same thing.

ANN: I'm sorry.

ERIC: Once upon a time I had a great life with him, you know, but I couldn't see it. And now it's too late. I can't go back to him.

ANN: Do you think it's always too late to go back?

ERIC: I don't know.

MOE: "Always". So black and white.

ERIC: Meantime, I crushed my fiancée.

ANN: The one you left at the altar?

ERIC: I mean, I guess I should go back and tell her I'm sorry, right? Ask her to forgive me.

ANN: I wouldn't do that if I were you.

ERIC: Why not?

ANN: You've already hurt her enough.

ERIC: But I need to know that she's alright and that it's O K for me to move on. I need to start a new chapter, you know? Again and again and as many times as it takes until I get it right. I mean, if I can't have a happy ending I can at least try for a new beginning, right?

ANN: So forgive yourself. Know that what you did was wrong and get on with your life. She'll be O K.

ERIC: How can I be sure?

ANN: I don't think you can be sure.

ERIC: Well...thanks. Good luck. It was good running into you. I was just going to see about a room.

ANN: A room? I sure could use a good place to sack out for a couple of nights.

MOE: Might I recommend Moe and Flo's Bed and Breakfast. Accommodations fit for a Queen.

ANN: Really? Thank you. Thank you very much.

MOE: Right on out through there.

(ANN *and* ERIC *exit. Beat.* MAX *enters.*)

MOE: Mornin'. Coffee?

MAX: Thank you.

MOE: Know what you'd like?

MAX: Yeah, um...

MOE: Stack a pancakes. Side a bacon. Maple syrup gently rolling over the top of yer cakes and just...kissing yer side of bacon?

MAX: Yeah. That'd be great.

MOE: Comin' up.

MAX: Do you have a kid?

MOE: Me? Yeah, sure.

MAX: How old?

MOE: Two.

MAX: What's his name?

MOE: Moe.

MAX: Moe Miller?

MOE: That's me.

MAX: Isn't that him?

MOE: That's little Moe.

MAX: Gotcha. Say, uh, how far am I from New York?

MOE: Where'd you start?

MAX: Seattle.

MOE: I'd say you're about halfway.

MAX: Thanks.

MOE: Still gotta cross the Mississippi up ahead. Why you headed to New York?

MAX: I'm looking for this woman. We had this great electricity together, and then she suddenly...left out of the blue.

MOE: And you want to find her, tell her you love her, and have a nice happy, fairy tale ending.

MAX: Yeah. I guess I kind of do. You think that's stupid?

MOE: No. Not at all. We all want that, don't we?

MAX: I quit drinking. That's a good sign, right? I mean for our future together.

MOE: Good as any.

MAX: I hope I can find her.

MOE: Oh, you'll find her. True love always wins out in the end. If...

(DAVE *enters and sits at the counter.*)

MOE: Mornin'. Coffee?

DAVE: Fuck me, yes. Please.

(MOE *pours the coffee.*)

DAVE: Thank you. Would you pass the milk? Can you tell me how far I am from Seattle?

MOE: Where'd you start?

DAVE: New York.

MOE: I'd say you're about halfway. Still gotta cross the Mississppi up ahead.

MAX: I'm from Seattle.

DAVE: My fucking car just broke down.

MAX: Really? What's wrong with it? Maybe I could take a look at it.

DAVE: Are you a mechanic?

MAX: No, but I'm pretty handy.

MOE: Do you know what you'd like?

DAVE: Um...Oh, I don't know, I guess I'll have...

MOE: Stack a pancakes. Side a bacon. Maple syrup gently rolling over the top of yer cakes and just...kissing yer side of bacon?

DAVE: Yeah, that would be great.

MAX: Why are you going to Seattle?

DAVE: To find my wife.

MAX: Really, I'm going to New York to find my girlfriend.

DAVE: Small world.

MAX: You think she'll come back? Your wife?

DAVE: She has to.

MAX: I'm sure she will. True love always wins out in the end. Right, Moe?

MOE: Oh, boy.

MAX: What's she doing in Seattle?

DAVE: I don't know. She's confused. I'm confused. She was one of the most brilliant lawyers I've ever seen, I mean, if she wants to be a potter or whatever, that's fine, but she doesn't belong out there. She belongs with me. It's just a fact.

MAX: Hmm...well, maybe she needed to leave to appreciate what she already had. (*He takes the letter out of his pocket.*)

DAVE: Mmm, maybe so. (*He takes the letter out of his pocket.*) Maybe I needed her to go to see how much I need her to stay. My name's Dave by the way.

MAX: Yeah. I know.

DAVE: I'm sorry...?

(KING *enters, carrying a "Missing" poster.*)

KING: Excuse me, kind people. I'm looking for my wife and son, who have run away due to a grave misunderstanding. I have been searching high and low for nigh on seven years. I would be most grateful for any information.

MOE: Pardon my asking, but...aren't you the King?

MAX & DAVE: The King!?

KING: Why, yes. I am the King.

MOE: My Lord, if you'll pardon my saying so, you look terrible.

KING: I have been wandering for nigh on seven years in search of my wife.

MOE: Your wife the Queen?

KING: But of course my wife the Queen. Who else?

MOE: But, my Lord, what incredible fortune. Why, she's...

(MAIDEN *enters, carrying her silver hands in her real hands.*)

MAIDEN: It is a miracle! My hands have grown back. First as baby hands, then as little girl hands, and now miraculously restored as my full-grown hands.

KING: My Queen?

MAIDEN: Uh...no. Must be someone else. Me not Queen. Queen killed and...uh, eyes poked out. Confirmation. Tongue too. Yech. Me not her. Nuh-uh.

KING: No, no, my Queen. My mother told me everything. It was all a grave misunderstanding. The work of the Devil.

(ANN *enters.*)

KING: I have searched high and low for you for nigh on seven years. At last we are together again.

MAIDEN: Oh. Thank goodness. You found me and now we can be together. Joy at last. I will introduce you to your son and we shall live happily ever after.

ANN: Oh...my...God.

MAX: Ann.

DAVE: Ann. Ann? How do you know my wife?

ANN: Dave, Max. Wait.

MOE: Gentlemen, please.

DAVE: You're not the guy with the furniture and the big dog!?

MAX: Look, I...

ANN: Boys, don't.

KING: Cease!

(DAVE *and* MAX *cease.*)

KING: Now then, young maiden, these two princes are obviously willing to compete for your hand. But only you can decide who is the proper suitor. Only you can determine what will bring you happiness.

(ANN *lookes them both over. Surveys the situation.*)

ANN: Oh, God. Why can't I have my happy ending handed to me like you two?

KING: Handed to us?

MAIDEN: That's not funny.

KING: You think this was easy? I have searched high and low for nigh on seven years. I have gone without sleep. Without food nor drink. I'm pretty fuckin' tired and hungry. No one gave this to me. I sacrificed. I made this happen. I had to outwit the Devil himself. Jiminey, I hate it when people make these things seem easy.

ANN: O K. Fine. But that's just you. What about her?

MAIDEN: Me? I had my hands cut off. I had to leave my family. I was almost killed by the King. I have been wandering for years and years guided by nothing but faith. I have suffered beyond belief.

ANN: But the last time I saw you you had nothing, now you have everything. You found your Prince Charming. A man willing to sacrifice for you. A man who truly loves you.

KING: And what do you have before you? Prince number one...

MAX: Ann, we were headed for such a wonderful life. Building the house. Don't you want that? How could you throw that away to go back to something that wasn't making you happy?

KING: Prince number two...

DAVE: Ann, I have always loved you. Since we were...kids, really. I want you back so desperately. We just have to make sure that we don't get complacent or take each other for granted. We've been married for ten years. We have to respect that and try again.

KING: Maiden...

ANN: I don't think you can do it. It's too much work.

DAVE: Then we'll make it our life's work.

ANN: What about the plan?

DAVE: We'll throw out the plan. I don't care about the job or the apartment or New York.

MAX: It's bullshit.

DAVE: I'll throw it all away if I have to.

MAX: Habits are too hard to break.

DAVE: I came running after you. Just picked up and left. We need each other.

MAX: You'll end up right back where you were, you know that.

DAVE: Please, Ann.

MAX: But you and I can do anything together.

ANN: Cease! Max...I'm married. You can't fill in what's missing in my life any better than that stupid fantasy house could. Only I can do that. Even if you are Prince Charming, the maiden is right, there are no guarantees. No guarantees that I would be happy with you. No guarantees that I will be happy with Dave. Just faith. A lot of faith and a lot of work.

MAIDEN: A lot of work.

KING: And sacrifice. Don't forget sacrifice.

MAX: There's nothing I can say to change your mind?

ANN: No.

MAX: You gave me hope, you know? 'Cause after Sharon died I just thought it was all over for me.

ANN: But it's not.

MAX: I don't know, Ann. I don't know.

ANN: You're a beautiful man. With a lot of love to give. It was a nice fantasy. With you, it was a very nice fantasy. But now we both have work to do. I have to keep building my marriage, and you have to start building your new house. (She crosses to DAVE).

(ERIC enters.)

DAVE: So you're coming back?

ANN: I was standing there, you know? Surrounded by a world of possibilities, and the phone was ringing. And I closed my eyes and tried to imagine perfection. I could have anything I wanted. Any whim immediately fulfilled in my mind's eye. I blinked and was surrounded by my perfect pottery. Blinked again and was surrounded by my perfect poetry. But in every imaginable permutation of perfection, I kept seeing you standing there with me. The two of us as kids filled with hope. That's all I've ever wanted.

DAVE: I love you.

ANN: I love you. And I'm sorry I left you like that. That was hurtful and irresponsible, but it was something I had to do.

DAVE: I know.

ANN: I want the world to be open for us. And I need you to hear me.

DAVE: You've opened my ears, believe me.

(The MESSENGER enters.)

MESSENGER: Alright. Mail's here. Got some messages to deliver. One for you.

(The MESSENGER hands an envelope to ANN, which she opens.)

DAVE: What is it?

(ANN removes a hundred-dollar bill and reads the back of it.)

ANN: "For the true winner." *(She tears it in two and hands half to DAVE).*

(DAVE pops his half in his mouth and begins to chew. ANN does the same. They exit.)

MESSENGER: One for you.

(MESSENGER hands a letter to MAIDEN, which she looks at.)

KING: What is it, my queen?

MAIDEN: It is from my father. We should visit him. I think he just might make a good grandfather.

(They exit.)

MESSENGER: And one for you. *(She gives ERIC a piece of pink stationery that has been taped together)*

(ERIC looks at it for a beat. He smiles. He sits.)

MAX: What does yours say?

MOE: It says have a cup of coffee and get on with your life.

(Blackout)

END OF PLAY

NOTIONS IN MOTION

inspired by Luigi Pirandello

A NOTE FROM THE PLAYWRIGHT

O K, here's the truth: I had received a number of reviews in which my work was compared to Pirandello's. But the thing is—I was barely familiar with Pirandello. I had read SIX CHARACTERS IN SEARCH OF AN AUTHOR in college, but that was about it. So I figured hey, better read up on the guy.

In August 1996 I started reading his plays, which I really liked and which I though suited adobe very well. The problem was that some of them were hopelessly dated. adobe had never done a "period" piece, and I wasn't sure that we wanted to.

As the plots of Pirandello's plays were swimming through my head, I read an article in *The New York Post* which seemed strikingly similar to the plots of Pirandello. I decided that without doing any research into the "truth" and "facts" behind the article, I would adapt Pirandello with this article as my guide.

The article recounted the death of a Mafia heir apparent. It seems that this guy (you may remember the case, but if you don't there's no use naming real names) was meant to marry some socialite or other when he caught her cheating on him—with another woman. Rather than face dishonor with his family, the man pulled out a gun and shot himself on the spot.

These facts formed the foundation for my play. While this play is based on that article, let's face it—I made a lot of stuff up. The incident never made headlines, and other than the article I never heard anything more about it. I have no idea what the facts of the case were other than what I read in the paper, and so any similarities to persons living or dead are purely unintentional. (Isn't that what you're supposed to say?)

As for Pirandello, I took his three-act structure, basic themes, plot points, and characterizations and jumped off from there, doing a hell of a lot of modernizing along the way. Whatever the results— I hope you enjoy.

ORIGINAL PRODUCTION

NOTIONS IN MOTION was first presented by the adobe theater company, opening on 28 May 1997. The cast and creative contributors were:

DAVID . . . . Arthur Aulisi
LYDIA . . . . Kathryn Langwell
DON . . . . Adam Nelson
FREDDIE . . . . Henry Caplan
DELIA . . . . Stacy Leigh Ivey
PAULI . . . . Jay Rosenbloom
MICHELLE . . . . Beau Ruland
MAN . . . . Gregory Jackson
WOMAN . . . . Erin Quinn Purcell
GREGORY CANARONI . . . . Josh Manson

Director . . . . Jeremy Dobrish
Sets . . . . Matthew E Maraffi
Lighting . . . . Alex Radocchia
Costumes . . . . Erin Quinn Purcell
Video design . . . . J Mole

CHARACTERS

The cast:
DAVID, *an amateur philosopher*
LYDIA, *a very old matriarch*
DON, *a hot-headed romantic*
FREDDIE, *a simple smile. When angry, a rage with nowhere to go.*
DELIA, *a dramatic lover*
PAULI, *a cold killer*
MICHELLE, *a colder killer*

The interlude actors:
MAN
WOMAN

The audience:
ANNA
NELL
A
B
C
D
E

Cameo:
GREGORY CANARONI

(The audience is seated in the round in four sections. The STAGE MANAGER is visible behind a bank of computer equipment. There are four television monitors showing a live feed from the dressing room. These monitors will alternate from a long shot of the dressing room in general to a tighter shot of a dressing mirror in front of which various actors will prepare before going onstage. The monitors will stay on throughout the play, and the director should feel free to block actors in the mirror throughout the play at times when they are being spoken of onstage. There are two seats in the audience that are reserved. Shortly after the STAGE MANAGER calls "places", two women are escorted in by the house manager and shown to these "reserved" seats. As soon as they are seated the lights go to black. In the dark we hear the STAGE MANAGER's voice: "Act One. Scene One: A room in the home of Lydia Portes". The lights come up dimly on LYDIA, an old woman. We hear her voice.)

LYDIA: *(V O)* I am told they got into an argument. I heard they were ready to fight....I cannot have this.

(A buzzer buzzes as the lights pop on. LYDIA goes to the buzzer and speaks into it, "Yes?" DAVID's voice, "It's David". LYDIA buzzes him in. DAVID enters.)

LYDIA: David, thank you so much for coming.

DAVID: Of course I came, Mrs Portes. You sounded so upset on the phone.

LYDIA: David, let me say this: You have always been such a great help to this family. Ever since your dear mother passed away and I took pity on you, and took you in, you have become like my second grandson and like a brother to my dear, dear Donald.

DAVID: Thank you, Mrs Portes, I've always felt...

LYDIA: You have saved this family on a number of occasions with your calm, your patience, and your logic.

DAVID: That's very kind, Mrs Portes, but please, at the risk of offending, there's no need for flattery. Just tell me the problem. You know I'll do anything to help.

LYDIA: The problem? Oh yes, the problem. Alright. This is the problem:

(There is a stylized lighting change, and LYDIA addresses the audience. The following speech is spoken entirely in Italian. During this the various actors come out and pantomime LYDIA's descriptions.)

LYDIA: I am on the verge of a very important deal with the Canaroni family. A deal that stands to make me a lot of money. Now. Mrs Canaroni's dear, departed son, Gregory, was engaged to marry an outsider. Delia. The night

before the wedding, Gregory caught Delia cheating on him with a woman.
Michelle Rocca. Now. Michelle Rocca is not just any woman, she is the
woman Gregory's own brother was readying to marry. So Gregory
Canaroni finds his fiancée, Delia, in bed with his brother's fiancée, Michelle
Rocca, removes a gun, and kills himself. Now. The Canaronis have naturally
vilified Delia, which I myself must do in order to save my deal with them.
But.

(DON *and* FREDDIE *set themselves up at a table.*)

LYDIA: Last night my grandson Donald was out at a restaurant with his old
friend Freddie. From what I hear they got into a huge argument. Freddie
was saying:

FREDDIE: *(In Italian)* Delia manipulated Gregory's downfall. She's nothing
more than a scheming bitch.

LYDIA: *(In Italian)* But my Donald was saying:

DON: *(In Italian)* Delia did it for Gregory's own good. She was only trying to
save him.

LYDIA: *(In Italian)* If this is true, if Donald is on Delia's side of the argument,
I will be cut out of the deal with the Canaronis and lose a lot of money.

(*The lights restore, and* LYDIA *once again speaks English.*)

LYDIA: That is the problem.

DAVID: Mrs Portes, may be I be completely honest with you?

LYDIA: Of course, David.

DAVID: Well...I don't actually speak Italian.

LYDIA: What?

DAVID: I say that I don't actually speak....

LYDIA: Oh. The younger generation.

DAVID: Do you think you could...?

LYDIA: The whole thing?

DAVID: Well, it would help.

LYDIA: Alright. This is the problem:

(*There is a stylized lighting change, and* LYDIA *addresses the audience.
During this the various actors come out and pantomime* LYDIA's *descriptions.*)

LYDIA: I am on the verge of a very important deal with the Canaroni family
that stands to make me a lot of money. Now. Mrs Canaroni's dear, departed
son, Gregory, was engaged to marry an outsider. Delia. The night before the
wedding, Gregory caught Delia cheating on him with a woman. Michelle

Rocca. So Gregory Canaroni finds his fiancée, Delia, in bed with his brother's fiancée, Michelle Rocca, removes a gun, and kills himself. Now. The Canaronis have naturally vilified Delia, which I myself must do in order to save my deal with them. *But.*

(DON *and* FREDDIE *set themselves up at a table.*)

LYDIA: Last night my grandson Donald was out at a restaurant with his old friend Freddie. From what I hear they got into a huge argument. Freddie was saying:

FREDDIE: Delia manipulated Gregory's downfall. She's nothing more than a scheming bitch.

LYDIA: But my Donald was saying:

DON: Delia did it for Gregory's own good. She was only trying to save him.

LYDIA: If this is true, if Donald is on Delia's side of the argument, I will be cut out of the deal with the Canaronis and lose a lot of money.

(*The lights restore, and* LYDIA *is once again an old woman.*)

LYDIA: That is the problem.

DAVID: Shit, Mrs Portes, that is a problem.

LYDIA: What did you say?

DAVID: I say shucks, Mrs Portes, that *is* a problem.

LYDIA: You're telling me. And so, my dear David, I need you to talk some sense into my Donald. Get him away from that vile creature. I will take some money from the Canaroni deal and make it well worth your while.

DAVID: Mrs Portes, don't insult me, of course I'll help. You don't need to offer me any money. After all you've done for me, of course I'll talk to Don. I'll get him to side against Delia, don't you worry.

LYDIA: Oh, thank you, David. Because you know, if Donald is in love with Delia, I am sunk.

DAVID: Whoa, whoa, whoa. Who said anything about him being in love with Delia?

LYDIA: She cast a spell on Gregory Canaroni, and now she is casting one on my Donald.

DAVID: Mrs Portes, Don is not in love with Delia.

LYDIA: That is why he is defending her. It is the only thing that makes sense. Have you ever met her?

DAVID: Delia? Sure.

LYDIA: Is she pretty?

DAVID: Very.

LYDIA: Mmm-hmm. What does she do?

DAVID: She's an actress.

LYDIA: I knew it!!!

DAVID: Mrs Portes, she's really not all she's cracked up to be, believe me. She's like a frightened little child, to tell you the truth.

LYDIA: Aaah! What? Are you defending her now?

DAVID: I could make a case for her if I had to. Hell, she must have her own side of the story. Maybe that's all Don was saying. He probably got cornered in an argument and was just trying to weasel his way out.

LYDIA: I did not ask you here to placate me. I asked you here to get Donald away from that...that...that punta-bitch!

DAVID: Mrs Portes...

LYDIA: She is a disgusting animal, and my Donald was defending her. Explain that to me. For a woman to be doing those things with another woman?! It is revolting. How could she do that to Gregory Canaroni? He was such a nice boy. He had a sensitive soul. He was a painter. You saw his work. What did you think?

DAVID: Well...to tell you the truth, his subjects were good, but his brushwork left quite a bit to be desired. I mean, his skintones were accurate and everything, but nothing to write home about. Personally, I much prefer the work of...

LYDIA: Never mind. I cannot think about that right now.

DAVID: No. It's important, actually. You need a diversion.

LYDIA: A what?

DAVID: I say what you need is a diversion to take your mind off of Don. Here. Listen. A diversion about a diversion. Did I ever tell you what happened to me the night my mother died?

LYDIA: About a hundred times.

DAVID: I did? No, not this part of it. Listen. I'm sitting by her bedside. She's completely unconscious. And she has this weird thing where her eye won't shut. Even when she's asleep. She's blind in it of course, and it's just sort of caked open from lack of use. So it's like she's watching me all the time even though she's asleep, which is a pretty unsettling feeling. Anyway, I'm trying to distract myself from the uncomfortable necessity of sitting with her and I notice this bug swimming in her water glass. It had fallen in, and it was trying to swim its way out. It seemed to have complete faith that if it just kicked hard enough it could get itself out of there. I must've watched it for half an hour. Of course I knew that I could save it in an instant, but I just sat there and stared at it. I watched it die. My attention was so diverted by that friggin' insect that I missed the moment of my mother's death. Do you see my point?

LYDIA: David. Dearie. I have no idea what you are talking about.

DAVID: No? Hmm. It must seem a bit off the topic. But that's exactly the point. Tomorrow you'll see how funny all this is. You'll see how ridiculous it was to have been so worried over Don when I can steal your attention with a story about an insect. It's nothing for you to worry about. I'll take care of Don. If only I'd taken care of that insect. That insect that stole my attention while I missed the dying breath of my sainted mother.

(The sound of a buzzer. DAVID and LYDIA look at each other.)

DAVID: I hope that's not...

LYDIA: Donald!

(We hear the STAGE MANAGER's voice: "Interlude scene A. We find ourselves in a museum. Or perhaps an art gallery." LYDIA and DAVID get out of the way as MAN and WOMAN enter and compare two paintings.)

MAN: What do you think?

WOMAN: I have no idea.

MAN: You have no opinion?

WOMAN: Not really. I mean...well, what do other people say?

MAN: Like critics and stuff? Or just regular people?

WOMAN: I don't know. Critics, I guess.

MAN: It's hard to say. Some like this one. Some prefer that one.
The guy who painted that one is dead.

WOMAN: So?

MAN: Killed himself. Over a woman or something.

WOMAN: Does that make his paintings better?

MAN: Some people think so. What do you think?

WOMAN: I don't know. I don't want to say anything dumb. You obviously know more about it than I do, so why should I open my mouth and say something stupid when you obviously know all the intricacies and stuff?

MAN: Just tell me which one you like.

WOMAN: No. Knowing me, I'll just open my mouth and say something dumb only to find out later that someone else had a better opinion.

MAN: What does that mean? I just want to know what you think.

WOMAN: Yeah, but once you say something, once you put it into words or, God forbid, write it down, then you can't go back. You're stuck with it, and everyone judges you based on what you said. How does that saying go? "Better to keep silent and be thought a fool than to speak out and remove all doubt".

MAN: Don't worry about what anyone else might say, just tell me which painting you like.

WOMAN: But, see, I don't know that much about it. If I had all the facts about the painters and everything then maybe I could say better what I thought.

MAN: Well, you never have all of the facts about anything. So, in that case, why bother ever having an opinion?

WOMAN: I do have an opinion! I just told you.

MAN: Well, it seems like a pretty negative one.

WOMAN: Well, better a negative one than none at all.

(In the darkness we hear the STAGE MANAGER's *voice: "Act One: Scene Two. Back at the home of Lydia Portes".* MAN *and* WOMAN *exit as the lights return us to where we left off.)*

DAVID: If only I'd taken care of that insect. That insect that stole my attention while I missed the dying breath of my sainted mother.

(The sound of a buzzer. DAVID *and* LYDIA *look at each other.)*

DAVID: *I* hope that's not....

LYDIA: Donald!

*(*DON *enters.)*

LYDIA: Donald, thank goodness. What is going on? I have been hearing all sorts of things....

DON: *(Flipping out)* AAAAAARRRGGHHHHAAA IIIIIII...can't take it any more! Now my own grandmother!? Do I have to defend myself to every friggin' person I see? What did you hear? That I'm in love with Delia? That I'm obsessed with her? Out of my mind with passion? How the hell does word travel so fast? *(Notices* DAVID*)* Oh. Hey, David.

DAVID: Don.

LYDIA: Well, Donald, I think that you asked for it...defending that "woman" like you did. How could you?

DON: I didn't "ask" for anything. This whole thing has gotten blown completely out of proportion.

LYDIA: But some of the things you said...

DON: How do you know what I said? Were you there?

LYDIA: How dare you speak to me that way?

DON: I'm sorry. I need to calm down. Yes... you're right. I probably said some stupid things. I got a little drunk. I got a little carried away. Hey, forget about it; as far as I know, everyone's entitled to their own opinion.

LYDIA: No. You forget about it. Everyone is not entitled to their own opinion. Everyone is only entitled to my opinion! Isn't that right, David?

DAVID: Well, Mrs Portes...

LYDIA: The both of you. Putting up defenses for that...that...that punta-bitch!

DON: Grammy. Wait a minute. What...? "Both of you?" Were you defending her?

DAVID: Me? I just said I could put up a defense for her.

DON: And how would you defend her? I'd really like to know. I mean, I just want to see how your argument would stack up against the one I used against Freddie last night.

DAVID: I wasn't even there. I don't know what Freddie said.

DON: You want to know what Freddie said? Fine. This is what Freddie said:

(There is a stylized lighting change. DON *and* FREDDIE *set themselves up at a table.)*

FREDDIE: Delia set Gregory up. She *wanted* Gregory to catch her with Michelle Rocca, because she was trying to wrap Gregory up in a plot to get out of the prenuptial agreement.

DON: All I said was: *(To* FREDDIE*)* Delia couldn't have been plotting Gregory's downfall, because the worst thing that could have happened to Gregory would have been his marriage to a slut like Delia. If you want to put the blame on anyone, put it on Michelle Rocca, who is nothing more than a no-good, vicious cunt anyway.

*(*FREDDIE *exits. The lighting restores.)*

DON: If I got misunderheard that's not my fault.

DAVID: Well, if that's *really* all you said I don't see what harm's been done. *(To* LYDIA*)* Good?

LYDIA: *Bene.* Now go apologize to Freddie.

DON: No way!

LYDIA: Donald...

DON: Not after he fought with me like that.

LYDIA: But if you take Freddie's side, maybe I can still salvage the Canaroni deal.

DON: What does this have to do with the Canaroni deal?

DAVID: The Canaronis hate Delia, because they blame her for Gregory's death. If a Portes is siding with her, all bets are off.

DON: Oh. I see. I didn't think of that.

LYDIA: But if you and Freddie are on the same side against Delia...

DON: I understand.

LYDIA: So you'll do it?

DON: I can't.

DAVID: You said yourself, you and Freddie were just saying the same thing.

DON: But...

LYDIA: Donald.

DON: Do I have to apologize?

LYDIA: Please, Donald.

DON: Well...

LYDIA: It is my only way out.

DON: I know how important this must be to you, Gram-gram. So, you know.

LYDIA: You'll take Freddie's side?

DON: For you...

LYDIA: You would not lie to me.

DON: Grammy...

LYDIA: Well, then, it is settled. Thank goodness. What a relief. With you and Freddie on the same side against Delia, the Canaroni deal can still be saved. Oh. I feel about ten pounds lighter. Perhaps I'll stop for some chocolate on my way out. Thank you, David. Good work. You are an absolute genius.

DAVID: It was nothing. Really.

LYDIA: And, Donald, for coming to your senses. (To DON) I'll have to pick you up a nice little something. Some of those truffles you like so much maybe. Well, I am off to the Canaronis to save our deal.

DON: Goodbye, Grammy.

(LYDIA exits. Beat)

DAVID: So now that she's gone, tell me the truth.

DON: About what?

DAVID: You weren't actually defending Delia last night just like everybody says?

DON: No. I told you...I got misunderheard.

DAVID: Misunderstood.

DON: No. Misunderheard.

DAVID: Uh-huh.

DON: Uh-huh what?

DAVID: Well, it just seems that if that was really all you said, you would have just laughed at what everyone else is saying. You wouldn't have gotten so pissed off.

DON: What!? Oh, so now you think I'm in love with Delia too?

DAVID: I didn't say that.

DON: I just told you, I'm agreeing with Freddie now.

DAVID: Well, sure.

DON: Right?

DAVID: Yeah.

DON: O K then. *(Pause)*

DAVID: But, you know, it could be that you're only siding with Freddie because you're mad at yourself for getting carried away with what you said last night.

DON: No I'm not, I'm doing it for Grammy. *(Pause)*

DAVID: But, you know, it could be that that's just a convenient excuse. Can't you see what's going on in your own mind?

DON: Oh, perhaps you'd like to enlighten me about my own mind, you know so much.

DAVID: Well, maybe you're taking Freddie's side against Delia because you don't want to own up to the true feelings inside of you.

DON: Bullshit!

DAVID: Don...

DON: It's a load of crap!

DAVID: Maybe last night you felt these feelings a little more than you'd care to acknowledge, and they got the best of you.

DON: That's not true.

DAVID: Come on Don, who am I? I'm on your side. I'm only trying to help you. I just spent half an hour lying up and down to your grandmother on your behalf, and now you don't even have the decency to own up to the truth?

DON: I'm telling you....

DAVID: Not even to yourself?

DON: Just wait 'til I talk to Freddie, then we'll see what I said.

DAVID: You said more than you wanted to, and now you want to take it all back. It's true, even if you won't admit it, it's still true. An illegitimate thought is just as real as an illegitimate child.

DON: What the hell is that supposed to mean!?

DAVID: It's like we're married to our thoughts, right? Don't you think? We take a side and we stick by it. But, then, sometimes we think certain thoughts that don't quite fit in with our usual game plan. And sometimes we mess around with some of these dirty little notions, huh? And from these little affairs are born thoughts and actions we would prefer not to face. But our thoughts and actions have consequences. Real consequences. And, so, here you are rejecting this poor little orphaned notion of yours, which has come knocking on your door despite your denials.

DON: Oh. That's funny. Very clever.

DAVID: Don't get defensive. All I'm saying is that you're more complicated and conflicted than you're letting on. We all are. Me too. Here...how 'bout this? A complicated and conflicted story about complicated and conflicted feelings. I ever tell you what happened to me the night my mother died?

DON: I thought your mother died like ten years ago.

DAVID: More. So what. I'm sitting by her bedside with her, right? And she's barely recognizable. The cancer has turned her body into some sickly shell of its former self, and I'm listening to her breathing, which is more like this disgusting rattling wheeze. And do you know what I'm thinking as she's laying there dying? I'm thinking, "Jesus Christ, will you please shut the fuck up with that horrible, ghastly wheezing". Nice, right? So what happens? I seem to get my wish. The wheezing stops. I felt sick to my stomach. Like I had been caught in a crime. So I bend over her to see if she's really dead. And there's a mirror hanging on her bedroom wall, and I catch a look at myself in the mirror and do you know what expression I see coming back at me? Joy and relief. What kind of son am I? Joy and relief, for Christ's sake. And then she started breathing again. And I started to cry. Cry like a little baby. Weeping my eyes out. Tears of joy and relief. And the kicker is that through the whole thing, all I could think was "I want my mommy". Do you see my point?

DON: You know something, David, I love you like a brother. But sometimes you get a little wound up, and I gotta admit, I don't know what the fuck you're talking about.

DAVID: Too complicated and conflicted, huh? But that's exactly the point. Feelings aren't always black and white. It's almost funny. It wasn't as funny for me, though, to wish my mother dead and need her so desperately at the same time.

DON: And what does this have to do with me?

DAVID: Take a good look at it, Don. There can be no doubt. You're in love with Delia.

DON: What?

DAVID: Madly, hopelessly in love.

(A buzzer buzzes.)

DON: Hold that thought. Hello?

(FREDDIE's voice: "It's Freddie".)

DON: It's Freddie.

(DAVID and DON look at each other. We hear the STAGE MANAGER's voice: "Interlude scene B. We find ourselves on line at a voting booth. Or perhaps on line at an A T M machine." DON and DAVID get out of the way as MAN and WOMAN enter.)

MAN: Who are you going to vote for?

WOMAN: I'm not sure.

MAN: Really? You mean, you don't just automatically vote for the Democrats?

WOMAN: No. Why? Do you do that?

MAN: Sure.

WOMAN: Don't you think that's a bit closed-minded?

MAN: Closed-minded? No.

WOMAN: Well, how do you know that the Democrats are automatically better?

MAN: Because they belong to my party, so they uphold my principles. It's like a good friend. You know he's going to side with you no matter what.

WOMAN: I can't believe you do that.

MAN: I can't believe you vote against what you believe in.

WOMAN: That's not what I do. I look at the actual people, not some high-minded principle that probably has no basis in reality anyway.

MAN: What?

WOMAN: You don't just support your friend automatically if she's saying something stupid. I hear the candidates out on various topics and form an opinion based on what I've heard.

MAN: You mean to tell me you actually believe all that campaign bullshit? You know that once they get elected they're just going to do what they want anyway. You willingly believe a lie.

WOMAN: No.

MAN: Yes.

WOMAN: Well...yes. O K. You're right. So I do. So what? People willingly believe lies all the time.

MAN: Why would anyone do that?

WOMAN: Because it's easier. Because sometimes lies are more pleasant to believe than reality. Especially when it's a lie about yourself.

MAN: That's ridiculous. Anyone who can't face up to the truth has a big problem.

WOMAN: That seems like a pretty negative opinion.

MAN: Well, better a negative opinion than none at all.

(We hear the STAGE MANAGER's *voice, "Act One. Scene Three. Back at the home of Lydia Portes." The lights return us to where we left off.)*

DAVID: Take a good look at it, Don. There can be no doubt. You're in love with Delia.

DON: What?

DAVID: Madly, hopelessly in love.

DON: What!?

(A buzzer buzzes.)

DON: Hold that thought. Hello?

*(*FREDDIE's *voice: "It's Freddie".)*

DON: It's Freddie.

DAVID: I heard.

DON: Well...now...I'll show you whether or not I'm in love with Delia.

*(*FREDDIE *enters.)*

DAVID: Freddie.

DON: *(To* DAVID*)* You shut up.

FREDDIE: Oh, hey, David.

DAVID: What did I say?

DON: Freddie, look...about that thing we...

FREDDIE: No, please. Let me. Don, I came to apologize for the fight we had last night.

DON: No way. I was just going to apologize to you.

FREDDIE: Really? Oh, what a relief. *(He hugs* DON.) Do you realize we were on the verge of throwing away a lifelong friendship?

DON: Oh, come on, it wasn't as bad as that. But, listen, about all those things I said last night. I don't think there's any need to....

FREDDIE: Well, I think it was as bad as that. I was up all night going over it. I can't believe I couldn't see how right you were.

DON: No, no, no, but...see, I wasn't...

FREDDIE: I really thought Delia was a manipulative bitch. I had a strong case for it too. But I always see people in such a harsh light, you know? And your point of view was so generous. I was just being...

DAVID: Generous? Really? You found his defense of Delia to be generous?

DON: No. I wouldn't say generous.

FREDDIE: You're right, generous isn't even a strong enough word. And, hey, he really stuck to his guns, even with everyone coming down against him. I've never seen you fight with such passion.

DON: Y...well, you were the one coming down the hardest, but, now, you know, you really don't need to...

FREDDIE: No. It's true. I wasn't even listening. Just arguing. I couldn't hear what you were saying, but it's so obvious. Delia's not nearly as bad as I thought. You have me totally convinced.

DON: Will you just shut up?

DAVID: So you're taking Don's side?

FREDDIE: Absolutely. And I would defend Delia to the hilt.

DON: Jesus Christ, you fucking idiot!

FREDDIE: What? I just said I think you were right.

DON: Exactly. That's why you're an idiot.

DAVID: *(To* FREDDIE*)* He was just going to tell you that you were right.

FREDDIE: That I was right?

DAVID: Yup. That you were right in your *accusations* of Delia.

DON: And now you have the nerve to come around here and tell me you think I was right? Get the fuck out of here.

FREDDIE: Well, I thought about what you said.

DAVID: And he thought about what you said.

FREDDIE: And now he thinks I was right?

DAVID: Yeah, but you think he was right.

DON: Great. First you get me into an argument with a bunch of people who think I'm wrong, then you get me mocked for what I have to say. You get Grammy all flipped out over the whole thing. Then you shoot your mouth off about what "really" happened last night. Fucking great.

FREDDIE: You're blaming me for this?

DON: You're damn right I am! You provoked me. That's what happened. You know you did. You got me saying all sorts of stuff I never would have said without you egging me on. Stuff I didn't really mean. So, now, don't you dare go around saying you agree with me!

FREDDIE: But I do agree with you.

DON: You idiot!

FREDDIE: You were right, what you said.

DON: Shut up! Idiot! I had this all worked out. I don't care what you say. I agree with you, damn it! You were right. You were right, you were right, you were right. So there, you fucking idiot.

FREDDIE: You better stop calling me an idiot.

DON: How can I? It's all you fucking are is a total and complete fucking idiot.

FREDDIE: I come here to apologize to you....

DON: Idiot.

FREDDIE: To agree with you...

DON: Idiot.

FREDDIE: And you call me an idiot?

DON: *I-di-ot.*

FREDDIE: I'm warning you.

DON: Idiot! Idiot! Idiot!

FREDDIE: I'm serious.

DON: Fucking, total, stupid, fucking idiot.

FREDDIE: Fine! That's how you feel about it, Mr Bigmouth?! We'll see who's the fucking idiot! (*He storms off.*)

DAVID: Freddie...wait, no, come on, don't leave like that. Oh, this is a disaster.

DON: Let him go.

DAVID: You know the way Freddie overreacts. He's liable to do something stupid. Or worse, go to Pauli. I didn't mean for him to... I was just trying to get you to face up to the truth.

DON: Well, maybe you should stay out of my business.

DAVID: No, I've got to do something to keep the situation under control. Maybe tell him a story. I'm going after him. (*He exits.*)

DON: Stay out of my business! (*Pause. He is alone onstage.*) Stupid idiot.

(*The buzzer buzzes.*)

DON: Now who the fuck could that be?

(*We hear the* STAGE MANAGER's *voice: "Interlude Scene C. We find ourselves at a bar. Or perhaps in a nightclub."* DON *gets out of the way as* MAN *and* WOMAN *enter and dance.*)

WOMAN: So, what did you think?

MAN: I only met him very briefly.

WOMAN: Well, first impressions are very important. Once someone forms an opinion about you it's very hard to change it. So, did you think he was cute?

MAN: Sure, I guess so.

WOMAN: Doesn't he have a sad sort of smile?

MAN: A sad sort of smile? Actually, now that you mention it...yeah, he sort of did.

WOMAN: I know.

MAN: Or maybe I'm just seeing that now in hindsight. Maybe he just had sort of a neutral face.

WOMAN: He kisses like a dream. Did he say anything...?

MAN: You mean...?

WOMAN: ...about me?

MAN: He was pretty quiet, actually. It didn't seem like he knew the other guys there too well, so he just sort of hung back.

WOMAN: No, he was quiet because he knows. He knows how much people hurt each other with their words. Unless you're a hundred percent sure of what you're saying you better just keep your mouth shut. He told me that. *(Pause)* So...did he say anything? About me?

MAN: You know, I honestly don't remember. I don't think so, though. The high point of the evening was actually an argument that broke out.

WOMAN: Yeah?

MAN: Between these two other guys. I didn't catch most of it. But it was definitely over a girl. One guy saying she was a manipulative bitch and the other generously defending her.

WOMAN: That's very interesting. Well...so, did you get to talk to him at all?

MAN: Who?

WOMAN: Who!?

MAN: Oh, right. Sorry. Uh, a little.

WOMAN: Well, what were you talking about?

MAN: Just stuff. I remember...what was it? Wait, it wasn't him, though, I don't think, but somebody said, "Women are like dreams, they are never quite what you expect them to be."

WOMAN: But he didn't say that?

MAN: I don't...think so. No.

WOMAN: Are you sure?

MAN: I don't really remember that well. I had a lot to drink.

WOMAN: Oh, God, now I'm wondering if I'm making a big mistake. Maybe I shouldn't see him anymore. Or maybe...you know how I'm always so nice to him? Maybe I need to be a little nastier.

MAN: No. Don't do that. You should always just be yourself.

WOMAN: But who am I, really? I don't know. One minute I'm laughing and having a ball. The next minute I'm off crying in the corner. What is that? It's a nightmare, really.

(We hear the voice of the STAGE MANAGER: *"Act One, Scene Four. Back at the home of Lydia Portes". MAN and WOMAN exit as the lights return us to where we left off.)*

DON: Stupid idiot.

(The buzzer buzzes.)

DON: Now who the fuck could that be? *(To the buzzer:)* Hello?

(DELIA's voice: "It's Delia".)

DON: Holy shit. What the... *(To the buzzer)* Uh...oh, O K.

(He buzzes the buzzer. After a beat DELIA *enters.)*

DON: Delia...I...wasn't expecting you.

DELIA: I just came to thank you for what you did.

DON: No, really, that was nothing. I was just...

DELIA: When I heard what you said...I can't tell you how I felt. I really began to recognize myself in your words. I saw who I am through what you said about me. You understand me in a way that I don't even understand myself.

DON: Uh-huh?

DELIA: Oh, it just sends shivers up my back. To be so fully understood. I've never felt anything like that.

DON: Well, that's great. Because, you know, it really just...whew. I mean, I just had a glimpse into your mind, I guess. Just a, like a...very fleeting glimpse and then...whew...later it really just went out the window.

DELIA: It did?

DON: But never mind. I mean, if you say that that was you. That you recognized yourself...

DELIA: Oh, absolutely.

DON: Then I guess I have to stick to what I said last night, God help me.

DELIA: I honestly don't know how you did it. I mean, you managed to see the real me. The real me who I always seem to be chasing. Wanting to catch her and ask her what she wants, or why she's crying, or how she can find peace.

DON: Mmm. Yes, you could certainly use a little peace. We both could.

DELIA: No one else understands me. Not even Gregory. I still see him, you know. Gregory's face. The way it was just before he blew it off. Red hot with passion and then suddenly drained white of blood. His body slumped and lay limp at my feet. He ended his life over a useless nobody like me, and now I carry that around with me wherever I go. It makes me crazy. Can you imagine how I feel?

DON: I'm so sorry. You poor thing.

DELIA: I don't even know who I really am anymore. I'm just the person people expect me to be. Not myself. I look in the mirror and I don't see my self. Just useless make-up painted over a blank and empty mask. I've traded my face for a mask. Do you see?

DON: No. It's just that you can't see yourself the way I see you. There's so much goodness inside you. That's what I was trying to show people last night. You're just like a frightened little child.

DELIA: Isn't it funny to think sometimes that we were actually children once? I look at little kids and can't even imagine ever having been so innocent. And the more you try to get it back the more phony it becomes. You can't fake innocence. I know, I've tried, but it just doesn't work. All I want is one thing about myself that I know to be true without contradiction.

DON: Well, what about the love? All the love you have inside of you? You are so...beautiful.

DELIA: But is all I am how I look? Men can't seem to see past that. The only reason they even talk to me is to get me into bed. They can't see the real me. Not the way you could. Even Gregory was no different. All he really wanted was my body. It's not that he was mean about it. Just the opposite. But that only made it worse. How does that expression go? "An angel is far more infuriating to deal with than a devil."

DON: (Overlapping) ...infuriating to deal with than a devil." That's exactly what I said last night.

DELIA: I know. I'm quoting you. I knew that things wouldn't work between us and that, if I married Gregory, I'd only end up hurting him.

DON: But until I explained it...

DELIA: I really didn't know why I had done it. I couldn't even see my own motives. You were so right. You are my guardian angel. My protector.

DON: I am?

DELIA: Mm-hmm. Marrying Gregory would have been a disaster. Do you know that he wouldn't even let me meet his family? The big, bad Beef-A-Roni's. How could he really love me if he was too ashamed of me to introduce me to his family?

DON: That bastard. I'll kill him myself.

DELIA: But he's already dead.

DON: Exactly.

DELIA: And so that's why I did what I did with Michelle Rocca. I wanted him to see me having pleasure in a way he could never give me. To finally use my body against him. No matter how confident a man is, he knows in his heart that he cannot pleasure a woman the way another woman can. Men get so turned on by the idea of two women together until they actually meet a lesbian. Then they get so scared, and, threatened, they lash out. I mean, why can't two women just love each other? Love is love, isn't it?

DON: You're not a...? A...?

DELIA: No, of course not. Me? What do you think?

DON: No, it's just that you seem to know an awful lot about women being with other women.

DELIA: Donald. I am an actress. It is my job to know these things.

DON: But, even so, messing around with Michelle Rocca is dangerous.

DELIA: I knew the risks.

DON: Do you love Michelle Rocca?

DELIA: No! I told you. I only did it because I needed Gregory to see us, so I could get out of the marriage and save him. I'm telling you, it was my only way out.

DON: The only way out of a marriage that would have just made him miserable. Well, there you have it. I was right all along. You know, I'm smarter than I look. And you...you're very brave. God, I hate it when people underestimate me. I never should've turned back on myself. Stupid! And that idiot Freddie said I had it all wrong. I don't know why no one'll listen to me.

DELIA: But you speak the truth.

DON: I know. But everyone seems to think Freddie's right. That this was all a plot on your part to manipulate Gregory and his family.

DELIA: What!?

DON: Yuh-huh.

DELIA: But I heard he was saying I was in love with Michelle.

DON: What!?

DELIA: He wasn't?

DON: No. He said that you knew that sleeping with Michelle Rocca would be the one thing the family couldn't bear to have out in the open, because it's such a taboo.

DELIA: Well... he is right about that.

DON: Yeah, but Freddie, idiot that he is, said that by threatening to start a scandal you were trying to weasel your way out of the prenuptial agreement.

DELIA: I can see how that would make sense.

DON: No, but he said that you were going to use it as blackmail.

DELIA: And people believe that?

DON: Everybody...

DELIA: Well, that changes everything.

DON: Everybody thinks you did it for the money.

DELIA: Did it for the money?

(DELIA *stares off into space for a moment, then buries her head in her hands.* WOMAN *enters and stands in the corner unnoticed.*)

DON: Are you O K? What's wrong?

DELIA: I don't know. I'm so confused. I don't know what's true anymore. My head is swimming.

DELIA & WOMAN: Who am I, really? I don't know. One minute I'm laughing and having a ball. The next minute I'm off crying in the corner. What is that? It's a nightmare, really.

(WOMAN *exits.*)

DON: What are you talking about?

DELIA: Who can say what their own true motives really are? If everyone believes Freddie, then maybe he was right all along. Maybe I did do it for the money.

DON: WHAT!? So now you think Freddie was right!? But you just said I was r...

(*Suddenly* LYDIA *enters.*)

DON: Grammy!...I...I didn't hear you.

LYDIA: Donald. Oh my God, Donald.

DON: What's the matter?

LYDIA: Everyone is talking about it. It's Freddie. He is...you know how he gets. He is getting his gun and coming over here to teach you a lesson.

DON: What? Who said that?

LYDIA: Something about "He'll show you who's an idiot". (*Notices* DELIA) Oh my god. Is this her? Is this...that...punta...

DON: Yes, Grammy.

DELIA: Don't worry, Mrs Portes. I'll stop Freddie.

DON: No, wait.

DELIA: I just need to talk to him. (*She exits.*)

DON: Delia, wait...don't do anything stupid. Let me...just. Shit!

LYDIA: So, it is true?

DON: AAAAAARRRGGHHHHAAA IIIIIII...can't take it any more. What? What's true, Grammy? That I'm in love with her!? That Freddie's coming over here with a gun!? That this whole thing is over an argument no one can answer!? I don't know what the truth is. Neither does Freddie. Jesus Christ, even Delia doesn't know herself. She doesn't even know her self. I don't know what's true, Grammy. How can I know!?

(Blackout)

(We hear the voice of the STAGE MANAGER: *"End of Act One." Set change and/or intermission as appropriate)*

ACT TWO

(We hear the STAGE MANAGER'*s voice, "Act Two. Interlude Scene D. We find ourselves on a long car ride. Or perhaps in an airplane." Lights reveal* MAN *and* WOMAN.)

WOMAN: There's something I've wanted to ask you for a long time.

MAN: Yeah?

WOMAN: Are you gay?

MAN: What?

WOMAN: You heard me.

MAN: What do you mean?

WOMAN: What do I mean?

MAN: Yeah.

WOMAN: Well, whenever I see you with a woman, talking to her, or flirting with her, or whatever, nothing ever seems to happen. So I'm just wondering. A natural curiosity.

MAN: You want to know if I've ever slept with a man.

WOMAN: Yes.

MAN: No. I haven't.

WOMAN: So, then, you're not gay.

MAN: I didn't say that.

WOMAN: Well, if you've never slept with a man...

MAN: It's a little more complicated than that.

WOMAN: In what sense?

MAN: Well...maybe...I have slept with a man and I'm just lying to you right now.

WOMAN: Well, I can't very well make an informed decision about the truth if you're lying to me.

MAN: O K, O K, I've never slept with a man. But maybe I've...thought about sleeping with men.

WOMAN: That doesn't make you gay.

MAN: No? There are emotional issues too, you know, it's not just a sexual thing. What if I love men and am attracted to them but don't sleep with them?

WOMAN: So, all you've done is think about it.

MAN: Yes.

WOMAN: Well, that doesn't make you gay, does it?

MAN: You don't think so?

WOMAN: Just thinking about it?

MAN: Why not?

WOMAN: Because no one'll beat you up for that.

MAN: What?

WOMAN: Just kidding. I mean...all I'm saying is you won't be ostracized for what you think if you don't act on it.

MAN: So you're saying it's more of a life-style thing. You can't be gay without leading a gay life-style.

WOMAN: I didn't say that. Lots of people are gay, but they don't want people to know about it.

MAN: Yes, thank you, I believe I'm familiar with that.

WOMAN: So you're in the closet?

MAN: I...

WOMAN: No. Wait. You can't be in the closet. You have to have slept with a guy to be in the closet. All you've done is think about it, right?

MAN: Right.

WOMAN: Hmmm.

MAN: So, you think that means I'm not gay?

WOMAN: Well...why are you doing this to me?

MAN: Why is it so important for you to define me like that?

WOMAN: I'm not trying to define you.

MAN: Why can't I just be what I am?

WOMAN: Of course you are what you are. Duh. I'm just trying to get at the truth.

MAN: So, in your opinion am I gay or not?

WOMAN: I don't think being gay is something you can have an opinion about. You either are or you aren't.

MAN: Alright. So if it's so cut and dried, am I gay?

WOMAN: How am I supposed to know?

(We hear the STAGE MANAGER's *voice: "Act Two. Scene One. In the home of Freddie Sampson." The lights reveal* FREDDIE *pacing about his apartment, talking to* PAULI, *who is finishing a meal.)*

PAULI: You want me to take care of him?

FREDDIE: No.

PAULI: So, why am I here?

FREDDIE: I'll kill him myself. The fuck do I care.

PAULI: Freddie...

FREDDIE: At least shoot him in the kneecap. I'm so sick of his shit. Talk to me like that. Fuck him. He's out of his mind. He's calling me an idiot because I agree with him? So, now I gotta shoot him, because basically I think he's right and he thinks I'm right.

PAULI: *(Sarcastically)* Gee, that makes sense.

FREDDIE: No, it does make sense, you get two people running in opposite directions, they decide to swap paths, and, boom, you get a collision, right? The prosecution starts defending, and the defense starts accusing.

PAULI: Whatever. Oh, hey, Freddie, there was something I wanted to tell you.

FREDDIE: What?

PAULI: ...Uh, I don't know. I forgot.

FREDDIE: You know, I go over there, in good conscience, with only one thought in mind: to apologize.

PAULI: Yeah, but you didn't know....

FREDDIE: ...that he's in love with her. How was I supposed to know he was defending her because he's in love with her? What am I, a psychic?

PAULI: You don't look like a psychic.

FREDDIE: I thought we were just arguing, you know?

PAULI: Psychics wear those...turbans.

FREDDIE: If I knew he was all emotionally wrapped up in it, I wouldn't have come down so hard.

PAULI: Fuckin' Dionne Warwicke and whatever.

FREDDIE: Are you listening to me? Jesus. You know I make one false move, make one stupid mistake, and that's all anybody ever remembers. That's how I'm judged. Fuck that.

PAULI: Sucks.

FREDDIE: Of course he's all touchy about it. I tell him he's right, he calls me an idiot, and now I gotta put a bullet in him.

(The buzzer buzzes.)

FREDDIE: Hello.

(DAVID's voice: "It's David." FREDDIE buzzes the buzzer.)

FREDDIE: The fuck does he want?

PAULI: The fuck does he want?

(DAVID enters.)

FREDDIE: The fuck do you want?

DAVID: I just wanted to let you know how happy I am that you're going to teach Don a lesson.

FREDDIE: You are?

DAVID: Oh, hi, Pauli.

PAULI: What's up?

DAVID: *(To PAULI)* You're not gonna kill Don, are you?

PAULI: Not unless he asks me to.

DAVID: Oh, O K. That's good.

FREDDIE: So, why are you so happy that I'm going to teach Don a lesson?

DAVID: Well, you put a bullet in him, hell, I'm sure he'll put a bullet in you too. Do you both some good.

FREDDIE: Thanks a lot.

DAVID: Just a flesh wound, right? I mean you are old friends. Give you a little memento to remember this whole thing. But, hey, here's the real kicker. Guess who I heard showed up at Don's right after you left.

FREDDIE: Not Delia.

DAVID: Bingo.

PAULI: The broad?

FREDDIE: To thank him for sticking up for her.

DAVID: Well, yes, at first. But get this. When she heard what your arguments were last night, you know what I heard she did?

FREDDIE: What?

DAVID: She agreed with *you*.

FREDDIE: What!?

PAULI: Get out of here.

DAVID: Can you imagine? So, now, what are we going to do about Don?

FREDDIE: What do you mean?

DAVID: Well, you and Don switched sides, right? So now he has your original opinion against Delia, and you're left saying Delia was just trying to save Gregory, which Delia herself no longer thinks is the case.

FREDDIE: Um...well, I guess, hmm, I don't know, I guess I don't need to...

DAVID: Ah, ah, ah...careful. You can't change your mind back now. Delia needs a champion now more than ever. And you're just the guy to defend her. The one who originally accused her.

FREDDIE: Defend her against what? Her own accusations against herself?

PAULI: Against the guy who originally defended her?

DAVID: Exactly. You know, I completely respect Delia for changing her mind and accusing herself. That takes guts. I mean, look, who are you? Freddie. What do you do? Coupla odd jobs for the family. Occasionally get your hands a little dirty. Make enough to eke by. Who are you? Pauli. What do you do? You...well, you hurt people. Who am I? David. What do I do? Nothing really. Live off a trust fund and do my best to keep the rest of you out of trouble.

FREDDIE: What's your point?

DAVID: All we know about each other or ourselves are these little crumbs of reality we cling to. They didn't apply yesterday, and they probably won't apply tomorrow. Here. Look. A quick story about how quickly things change. I ever tell you what I did the night my mother died?

FREDDIE: Oh, Jesus.

DAVID: After she died her eye still wouldn't shut. It's caked open still, right, like she's still watching me even though she's gone. I needed to get some fresh air, so I take a walk by the park. I'm pretty depressed right, 'cause, you know, my mother just died. And all I can do is soak up the decay and rot around me. The smell of piss everywhere I turn. I'm wandering around thinking, "What does it all mean?" "What's the point?" I just wanted to blow my brains out. And then I pass this little kid on the street who looks just like me when I was a kid. Same haircut and everything. And he looks up at me and he smiles with this expression of pure innocence. And suddenly I look around and see where I am. I remember the last time I was standing on that particular corner when I was in love and life was great, and instantly I get all filled up with this incredible feeling of tenderness. Do you see my point?

PAULI: That you like to listen to yourself talk?

DAVID: I'm just trying to use an example from my life to help you guys understand what's going on. Jesus Christ, is metaphor as dead as my mother?

FREDDIE: But what in God's name are you trying to prove?

DAVID: Nothing. How can I? We can't prove anything. What do you really know for sure? Really? For sure? What do you really know for sure?

FREDDIE: And what the fuck does all this have to do with Delia?

DAVID: Don't you see what she's gone through? Everything's crumbled around her. She thinks you were right, for Christ's sake. Can you imagine? She's blaming herself. Hell, your entire notion of the world is nothing more than an opinion. But if your conceptions fall apart, you got nothing left. It's like waking up and discovering that nothing you thought about the world is true. That there is no truth. You'll see. It's not just her. It's you too. Just wait 'til she gets here.

FREDDIE: "She" who? Delia?

DAVID: No.

FREDDIE: Then who?

DAVID: Michelle Rocca.

FREDDIE: Michelle Rocca? She's in town...?

PAULI: (Remembering) Oh, geez...

FREDDIE: I thought she was in Chicago.

PAULI: ...Hey, Freddie, that's what I meant to tell you before. Michelle Rocca's in town. That chick's nuts. I heard she's here to kill Don. She'll do it too.

FREDDIE: So what does this have to with me?

DAVID: She'll try to get to Don before you do because of the nasty things Don said about her last night when he was defending Delia.

PAULI: Matter of honor.

FREDDIE: So?

DAVID: Don't you get it? It's you she's going to kill.

FREDDIE: Me? Why me?

PAULI: Yeah, why him?

DAVID: Because you and Don switched positions, right? Well, if you're really serious about all this, serious enough that you would put a bullet in an old friend, then you're the one who has to answer for all the insulting things Don said about Michelle Rocca last night.

FREDDIE: Are you out of your mind?

PAULI: No. He's right.

FREDDIE: So now I'm supposed to defend myself against Michelle Rocca?

PAULI: Not a chance. She'll wipe you out. And if she doesn't, the muscle her family has...forget about it.

DAVID: She's a desperate woman now that the marriage is off.

FREDDIE: Between Delia and Gregory?

DAVID: No. Between Michelle Rocca and Gregory's brother...Fredo Canaroni. They can't get married now that she was caught with Delia...

PAULI: He's right about that.

DAVID: And Delia just discarded her.

FREDDIE: Right. Delia discarded her!

DAVID: She used her.

FREDDIE: Used her. That's exactly what I said.

DAVID: Hey, hey, hey! I know you're upset here, and probably pretty angry, but you really can't go changing your mind back again.

FREDDIE: I'm not...Jesus Christ. I got nothing to hold onto here. Last night I knew what I thought was true—Delia's a manipulative bitch. Then Don convinces me I'm wrong. I try to be more generous. But then as soon as Delia admits she's guilty, proving that I was right all along, of course I want to switch back to my original opinion.

DAVID: But...

FREDDIE: But if I do that, I have to side with Don.

PAULI: Which you're not gonna do.

FREDDIE: I can't. I said I'd put a bullet in him, I can't back down from that now without welching on my word.

PAULI: Matter of honor.

FREDDIE: But if I was right the *second* time in my defense of Delia, then I got Michelle Rocca out for my head. I lose either way.

DAVID: Exactly. Now you got it. Boom. Gone. Just like that. Now you know what Delia's going through. Feels good, doesn't it?

FREDDIE: Good?

DAVID: It's exciting.

FREDDIE: Are you out of your mind? What the hell am I gonna do? I don't even know what I actually believe anymore. All these stupid opinions buzzing around my head.

DAVID: You're like a stick of wood tossed casually out to sea, floating on the currents of time and waiting for some random wave's whim to float you back to the steady comfort of the shore.

FREDDIE: No I'm not. I'll tell you what I am. I'm totally fucked is what I am. How the hell am I supposed to get out of this mess?

DAVID: O K, look, Delia definitely cheated on Gregory with Michelle Rocca. I'll even grant you that she used Michelle Rocca. I mean, Delia's probably been with other women, you know how those actors are. But Michelle Rocca? No way. So maybe she's curious. And Delia seduces her.

FREDDIE: Not hard to imagine.

DAVID: And so now Michelle Rocca's left open and vulnerable. Her pride is hurt. So what does she want to do? Deny reality, of course. "No, it wasn't like that. I didn't get used and hurt". What the hell else is she supposed to do? She can't take it out on Delia, because then she has to own up to what really happened. So she goes after Don and now, by extension, you.

PAULI: You know something? Fuck you. You come in here with this attitude about how nothing is real, anything can change, I don't even know what. Well, I don't want to hear it. You know why? Because if people are really as changeable as you say...I pity the whole stinkin' mess of us.

DAVID: We should be pitied. Look at the bullshit versions of ourselves we create just to save face so no one can see the fears, regrets, and inconsistencies that make up who we really are. Well, throw out the bullshit. You thought that when Don called you an idiot he was talking to you. He wasn't. He was talking to himself. You couldn't see it, but he was really talking to the bullshit version of himself that he can't see in himself, but which he saw mirrored in you.

(Pause)

FREDDIE: Wow. You're right.

PAULI: Wow. I'm still really hungry.

DAVID: And, because of that, you two are going after each other with guns? Come on, Freddie.

FREDDIE: Well...so what am I supposed to do?

(The buzzer buzzes.)

FREDDIE: The fuck is that? Hello?

(DELIA's *voice*, *"It's Delia".*)

PAULI: Whoa. Were you expecting her?

FREDDIE: No.

PAULI: Don't let her up.

FREDDIE: Why not? Should I?

DAVID: Might as well.

FREDDIE: I need to know what happened.

DAVID: Then talk to her.

FREDDIE: I need to get to the bottom of this.

PAULI: Don't do it.

FREDDIE: I need to know whether I was right or whether... I was right the second time. I'll go down and talk to her. *(To the buzzer)* I'll be right down. Wish me luck.

DAVID: Good luck.

(FREDDIE *exits. Pause)*

PAULI: So, what do we do now?

DAVID: I guess we wait. *(Long pause)* You want to hear a story? It's good, you'll like it.

PAULI: Yeah?

DAVID: Sure.

PAULI: What kind of story? Like a bedtime story?

DAVID: No, not like a bedtime story.

PAULI: Like a...you know like a scary, tell around the campfire story?

DAVID: No. A story. Just a story.

PAULI: Like about you?

DAVID: Yeah. You know, just a regular story about me.

PAULI: The story has girls in it?

DAVID: No, it's not a dirty story.

PAULI: So, how do you know I'll like it if it's not a dirty story?

DAVID: Look, it's just a story I think you'll like, you wanna hear it or not?

PAULI: Alright.

DAVID: *(Happy as a clam)* I ever tell you about the night my mother died...?

(MAN *and* WOMAN *enter. They are not in* DAVID *and* PAULI's *reality though all are onstage.*)

WOMAN: I'm a vampire.

MAN: What?

WOMAN: You heard me.

MAN: You're a vampire?

WOMAN: Yes.

MAN: Fuck you, you're not a vampire.

WOMAN: I'm serious.

MAN: You want a beer?

WOMAN: Why don't you believe me?

MAN: Because you're not a vampire.

WOMAN: Last night, when I was sleeping, a dark man in a cape entered my room. I have no idea how he got there. I was scared but somehow sort of paralyzed. He leans down to my half-asleep body and sweeps me up in his arms. I can't tell you...I felt the most powerful sexual longing I've ever felt. He leans into my neck and he bites me. I could feel his teeth penetrating my skin. I screamed, but it was more from ecstasy than pain. The next thing I know he was gone. And now I'm terrified. I'm terrified that as soon as the sun goes down I'll turn into a blood-sucking beast.

MAN: Uh-huh.

WOMAN: On the other hand, I will be able to live forever. But in return I must kill people to survive. For my lifeblood. I mean, I guess I can kill the homeless, the despondent, the terminally ill. It's my choice. Although... I don't know, maybe I need fresh, pure blood. Hard to say. Anyway...either way the point is in order to become immortal, I have to turn immoral. But the reward is everlasting life. I'd spend my days looking for prey...and seeking out others like myself. I'm sure vampires prefer hanging out with other vampires. I'll start a vampire support network or something. What do you think?

MAN: Show me.

WOMAN: What?

MAN: The mark on your neck from where he bit you.

WOMAN: You mean the love bite of my master. Feast your eyes on this. (*She shows him her neck.*)

MAN: You are so amazingly full of shit sometimes.

(MAN *peels off the pieces of red plastic* WOMAN *has stuck to her neck.*)

WOMAN: Fuck you, you're so literal. Why does everything need to be "true"? Can't a girl just have some fun sometimes?

(MAN and WOMAN exit as DAVID and PAULI continue.)

PAULI: Nice story. (Pause) You hungry? You want to order up some Chinks or something?

DAVID: Sure.

(PAULI removes a cellular phone and dials.)

PAULI: Yeah. Hi. Order for delivery... Two-twenty-two Valesey Street... Number 2F... No, F, F, like fuck you... Gimme a beef with broccoli and a... (To DAVID) what do you want?

DAVID: They got chicken and cashews?

PAULI: Who am I calling here? Of course they got chicken and cashews. (To phone) And give me a chicken and cashews. (To DAVID) You want to split some dumplings or something?

DAVID: Yeah. Get the steamed vegetable.

PAULI: (To phone) Give me some fried pork dumplings.

(He hangs up. The buzzer buzzes.)

PAULI: That was quick. (He buzzes the buzzer.)

(MICHELLE bursts into the room.)

PAULI: Who the hell are you?

MICHELLE: Michelle Rocca.

PAULI: Doa! Uh. Very nice to meet you.

DAVID: Ah, Ms Rocca. We've been expecting you.

MICHELLE: Are you Freddie Sampson?

DAVID: No, I'm afraid you just missed him.

MICHELLE: Some bad things have been said about me by Don Portes. I know. I came here to even the score. But then I hear that I have an ally in Freddie Sampson.

DAVID: Well, I'm afraid he's just gone off with Delia. But there's something you should know about Freddie and where his opinions stand.

PAULI: Will you shut the fuck up?

DAVID: She has a right to know.

MICHELLE: Know what?

PAULI: Why do you like to stick your head up everybody's asshole and make everything so God damn difficult?

DAVID: I'm just telling the truth. Isn't that what everybody wants? The truth? Ms Rocca came here thinking Freddie is her ally, and I think she has a right to know that that's no longer the case.

MICHELLE: You mean he's taking her side?

DAVID: Mmm. And he's not the only one.

MICHELLE: You're taking her side too?

DAVID: Both of us.

PAULI: I fucking hate you.

MICHELLE: Well, sure. It makes sense. You've only heard her side of the story.

DAVID: Actually, none of us have heard her side of the story, not even Freddie.

MICHELLE: So how do you know I'm wrong? Especially Freddie, who originally sided with me. And so if he *has* switched sides, is he still after Don Portes?

DAVID: Well...it's a little bit tough to explain, but I guess Don and Freddie are still after each other because they've both changed their minds.

PAULI: No, that's not it at all. Freddie has a perfectly good and clear reason for going after Don. Don called him an idiot.

MICHELLE: I still don't see how it is that you all are turned against me without even hearing my side. How did that...bitch get you all on her side?

DAVID: Well, not all of us. There is one person who has turned against Delia.

MICHELLE: Who's that?

DAVID: Delia.

MICHELLE: She's turned against herself?

DAVID: Exactly.

MICHELLE: Maybe you could tell me where Freddie is.

DAVID: He just went off with Delia. That's all I know.

MICHELLE: Well, maybe I'll just wait. Maybe she'll turn up too. It might be good for us to see each other again. Yes. Indeed. You know this whole thing has been quite hellish for me. I can't explain to you...absolute hell. And all of this just to save Gregory. I loved him like a brother, you know? He would've been my brother-in-law.

PAULI: You tried to save him? By messing around with the bride right before the wedding?

MICHELLE: No. See? It wasn't like that at all. Let me explain. Gregory thought that by marrying Delia he could get her to stop sleeping around. But I knew that would never work. I was just trying to show him that anybody could have her, anytime, as lots of people had. She was the one trying to force him into a marriage that wasn't right for him.

DAVID: So you're not in love with Delia?

MICHELLE: In love with her? Are you nuts? Of course not.

PAULI: Whether you are or not, you still took her from him. You shouldn'ta done that.

MICHELLE: He bet me I couldn't.

PAULI: What?

DAVID: Who bet you?

MICHELLE: Gregory did. I'm telling you. Even his mother and Fredo were behind me. They couldn't stand that bitch. I tried to explain to Gregory that marrying Delia was a bad idea. That she was a slut. So he bet me that I couldn't prove it. His part of the bet was that if I could prove it he would call off the wedding. Instead he goes and kills himself.

PAULI: You took part in all of this?

MICHELLE: He challenged me. And the whole point was to save him.

DAVID: So who betrayed whom?

MICHELLE: The whole thing is awful.

DAVID: Really he betrayed you...

MICHELLE: Exactly.

DAVID: By killing himself!

PAULI: This is unbe-fucking-lievable.

MICHELLE: He knew what I was doing. I even said to him, "I'll bet given half the chance, she'd hop into bed with me". He was completely hooked. She's a vampire.

DAVID: Well, now, I wouldn't go that far.

MICHELLE: I'm telling you. That bitch is a fuckin' vampire. Once she gets her fangs in a person...

DAVID: She's not calculating enough to be a vampire. What sort of schemer tricks a man into marriage only to fall into bed with another woman?

(FREDDIE *enters.*)

FREDDIE: Oh...Michelle Rocca, I presume. What the hell are you doing in my apartment?

MICHELLE: I came to tell you...

FREDDIE: There is nothing you can tell me.

MICHELLE: Oh, there's a whole bunch I can tell you and you're gonna listen, see.

FREDDIE: Is that some sort of threat?

PAULI: Freddie...

MICHELLE: I've just been explaining to your friends....

FREDDIE: I don't care about your explanations.

MICHELLE: Well, before you go and put a bullet in Donald Portes....

FREDDIE: I'm not gonna put a bullet in Don.

PAULI: What?

DAVID: No?

MICHELLE: I knew it. She's caught him. She's got him right where she wants him. She's gotten him to promise not to shoot her precious knight in shining armor.

FREDDIE: Hey, what exactly do you want anyway? Come into my house talking all kinds of shit.

PAULI: Hey, back off of her, Freddie.

MICHELLE: So, now that you're over your problems with Portes, you want to start something with me.

PAULI: You can't fight her. So, what's the deal? Why aren't you going after Don now?

FREDDIE: I'm not going to add to that poor woman's misery just to settle my own stupid little score. The things she told me. My God. Do you know she's just like a frightened little child?

PAULI: Freddie! You said you would put a bullet in Don so you have to. It's a matter of honor. You back down now and your word is mud.

FREDDIE: But the whole thing is ridiculous. We're on the same side, for Christ's sake. You just like seeing blood and watching people get hurt.

PAULI: No, I... Well...yeah, that's true. But still...he insulted you.

FREDDIE: So? He called me an idiot. What's that between friends? The whole thing is bullshit. Let's just drop the whole mess.

PAULI: I can't believe you. You can't back offa Don after what you said. You just can't. Shit, I'll go over there myself and tell him that, if you won't put a bullet in him... I will! (He exits.)

DAVID: *(Calling after* PAULI*)* Pauli, calm down, will ya? Just give it some time to settle down. Shit.

FREDDIE: *(To* MICHELLE*)* As for you, why don't you follow his lead and get the fuck out of my apartment?

DAVID: I have to stop him. I know the perfect story. *(The buzzer buzzes.)*

FREDDIE: Now who the fuck is that? *(To buzzer.)* Hello?

(Voice from outside with Chinese accent: "Empire Szechuan".)

DAVID: Ooh. The food's here. Even better. *(Calling out the window)* Hey, Pauli, the food's here. Come on, the thing with Don can wait.

(FREDDIE looks at DAVID.*)*

DAVID: Me and Pauli got bored, so we ordered up some food.

FREDDIE: What'd you get?

DAVID: Beef with broccoli, chicken with cashews, and an order of dumplings.

FREDDIE: You get the steamed vegetable?

DAVID: Nah. Pauli wanted the fried regular.

FREDDIE: Ah well. Still. Sounds pretty good, I could use some food. *(To* MICHELLE*)* We're going to get the food. When we get back up, I expect to find you gone.

(FREDDIE and DAVID *exit.* MICHELLE *is alone onstage. She removes her gun and rubs it a little to clean it—maybe for luck. Puts it back. After a beat* DELIA *enters. She and* MICHELLE *look at each other for a good long time. They begin trembling with fear, passion, and raw emotion.)*

MICHELLE: Delia. Oh my God, Delia.

(She runs to DELIA, *and they embrace madly.)*

DELIA: Oh, Michelle. My beautiful Michelle.

(They kiss.)

MICHELLE: I couldn't stand being away from you. I need to be with you. Let's never be apart again.

DELIA: Never my love. Never. Everything is going so well for us. I've spoken with Donald *and* with Freddie. They are both on my side now. Can you believe it? They're both convinced I'm straight. So now, you don't need to get them to buy that ridiculous story about the bet....

MICHELLE: No. Listen. I've been thinking. I can't stand hiding the truth any more. I want to show the world my love for you. We don't need to hide this anymore.

DELIA: What? No. We can't. Things are going so well.

MICHELLE: But I love you.

(DAVID, FREDDIE *and* PAULI *enter with the Chinese food to see* DELIA *and* MICHELLE *still in an embrace.*)

DAVID: What the...?!

(*The Chinese food gets dropped on the floor.*)

FREDDIE: How can they?

PAULI: Where's my camera?

FREDDIE: With Gregory's death on their conscience.

DELIA: No. Let me go.

MICHELLE: You belong with me, in my arms.

DELIA: No, let go of me, I said.

FREDDIE: Hey, let her go.

MICHELLE: You keep out of this.

DELIA: Don't touch me.

(FREDDIE *and* PAULI *restrain* MICHELLE, *who is desperately trying to fling herself at* DELIA.)

DELIA: I'm not afraid of you! There's nothing you can do to me.
You could kill me and I wouldn't care.

MICHELLE: Delia! No. Please. I need you.

DELIA: I thought I felt sorry for you...or afraid...or something, I don't really remember. But now I just don't feel anything.

MICHELLE: Please, no. I'll go insane without you. (*To* PAULI *and* FREDDIE) Will you let me go!?

DAVID: I think she's already insane.

DELIA: Let her go. I'm not afraid of her.

MICHELLE: God, you are a vampire, the spell you have on me...but it doesn't matter, I want you. I need you.

DELIA: I'd rather be dead. I'd rather you killed me.

MICHELLE: How can you say that to me? I don't love you; I hate you.

DELIA: I hate you too.

MICHELLE: I'm completely filled with hatred. It's as if Gregory's spilt blood was coursing through my veins.

(She breaks free of FREDDIE *and* PAULI *and draws her gun. She points it at* DELIA, *then at the men. Then back at* DELIA. MICHELLE *drops the gun and runs towards* DELIA, *who runs away.)*

MICHELLE: Help me, Delia, please help me! I love you.

DELIA: No. Stay away from me. Don't touch me.

*(*PAULI *and* FREDDIE *again manage to restrain* MICHELLE.*)*

DAVID: Will you cut that out?

FREDDIE: For God's sake...

PAULI: I think I wet my pants.

DELIA: Why don't you just leave me in peace?

MICHELLE: Wait. I see now. Delia, please. Stop the act and listen to me. No more lies. Who cares what they think? Our love is all that matters. Why can't you just admit the truth?

DELIA: Yes, you're right. What am I doing? Of course you're right. It's all lies. All those things I said. Just to cover up our love. I have to be true to my self.

MICHELLE: You wanted me and I wanted you from the moment we lay eyes on each other.

DELIA: Yes! It's true. You're right. *(She runs to* MICHELLE *and flings herself at her, pushing* FREDDIE *and* DAVID *aside.)* I love you, my sweet Michelle.

MICHELLE: All we have now is each other. I love you more than anything. We have to be together.

DELIA: Always. We are so lucky. We have each other.

DAVID: It'll never last.

MICHELLE: Come, my love, let me take you away.

*(*DELIA *and* MICHELLE *exit in a flourish, swept away in passion.)*

PAULI: Will you get a load of that?

FREDDIE: They must be out of their minds.

*(At this point one of the women sitting in the audience who arrived late [*ANNA*] will get up from her seat and follow the actors playing* DELIA *and* MICHELLE *into the dressing room. She will be followed by the other woman who accompanies her [*NELL*]).*

ANNA: I can't listen to this bullshit anymore!

NELL: Anna!

(The actors onstage continue the scene, but with an awareness that something very weird has happened. From the dressing room we can hear ANNA *and* NELL *yelling,*

looking for someone. Any available staff [i.e., House Manager, Box Office Manager, Director] should pursue these women to the dressing room.)

DAVID: You think so? Well, what about you? At least they're not afraid to show how they truly feel.

FREDDIE: What the hell is that supposed to mean?

DAVID: Instead of judging them, why don't you learn from them and march on over to Don's and apologize?

FREDDIE: I got no problem with that. It's just that the food distracted me.

PAULI: No way. Don gets a bullet in him no matter what. *(The buzzer buzzes.)*

FREDDIE: Now who the fuck is that? *(To buzzer)* Hello?

(DON's voice, "It's Don".)

FREDDIE: It's Don. Alright now, let's just see who's afraid to tell the truth.

(DON enters.)

DAVID: Don.

PAULI: You shut up.

DAVID: What did I say?

FREDDIE: Don...

DON: No. Let me. Freddie, I just wanted to apologize for calling you an idiot.

(On the monitors we can see ANNA finding the actor playing DELIA, yelling at her, and punching her in the face. Many screams are heard from backstage. The actors onstage are very uncomfortable and desperately try to continue.)

FREDDIE: No way. Me too. Can't we just let bygones be bygones?

PAULI: No chance. *(He draws his gun on DON.)*

(ANNA and NELL come onstage to retrieve their belongings. The action onstage stops. The DIRECTOR [Or whomever] tries to escort them out.)

ANNA: I'm sorry, everyone, I'm sorry. But this bullshit. That's not me up there, and that's not Nell. I'm sorry.

(At length she is ushered out of the theater, and the actors onstage try to cover and resume the scene.)

DON: What the...?

DAVID: Pauli. Wait. Don't...

(FREDDIE draws his gun on PAULI.)

FREDDIE: Drop it.

PAULI: You gotta be kidding me.

(PAULI turns on FREDDIE. DON draws a gun.)

DON: Oh no you don't.

PAULI: What the...?

DAVID: Pauli, come on.

DON: Drop it.

PAULI: No chance. *(He alternates pointing his gun at DON and at FREDDIE.)*

FREDDIE: Come on, Pauli, drop it.

PAULI: Someone's getting a bullet in them, even it kills me.

DAVID: Oh, this is ridiculous. Listen. Guys, listen. Did I ever tell you about the night my mother died?

PAULI, FREDDIE, DON: *(All turning their guns on DAVID)* Shut up! *(They turn their guns back on each other.)*

(The actor playing DELIA can be seen leaving the dressing room and heading for the exit to the theater with an ice pack over her eye. She is pursued by the actor playing MICHELLE and various others, who are calling her by name, urging her to calm down, but it is no use. They all exit. The play is completely falling apart, the actors push on, trying to get to the end of the scene.)

DAVID: Sorry, O K, O K, look, Pauli, will you just drop the gun?

PAULI: Why do I have to drop it? Why don't you tell them to drop it?

FREDDIE: I'm not dropping it.

DON: I'm not dropping it.

DAVID: Come on, how about everyone drop it on the count of three.

PAULI: Who counts?

DAVID: Oh, for crying out loud.

(The buzzer buzzes.)

FREDDIE: Now who the fuck could that be? David, would you get that? I'm a little tied up right now.

DAVID: No problem. *(To buzzer)* Hello.

(GREGORY's voice, "It's Gregory Canaroni".)

DAVID: It's Gregory Canaroni.

DAVID & FREDDIE: Gregory Canaroni! I thought he was dead.

(Blackout)

(We are left in darkness for a good long time. Much activity is seen on the monitors. Actors can be heard in the dressing room. Tempers are flying. Nobody knows what's

going on. The people in charge [DIRECTOR, STAGE MANAGER, HOUSE MANAGER, etc] meet to discuss options. "What happened?" "Is Delia O K?" "Can she continue?" "Can someone else do her part?" etc. Actors come out and ask what's going on. At length the lights are brought up, and someone in charge comes onstage to make an announcement.)

DIRECTOR: Uh, Hi. Good evening, ladies and gentlemen. My name is *(Name)* and I'm *(Function)*. You know, there's a saying that live theatre is so exciting because anything can happen. And, as I think you just saw...tonight anything did. Um...we're just in the process of sorting a few things out with a couple of actors. I hope you'll be patient with us. I'm...well, really I'm just stalling, I guess. But we should be with you in just a moment. We're going to bring some music up. Thank you so much for your patience.

(Another conference takes place: "What's the news from Delia?" "What do you mean she won't go on?" "What are we going to do?" "No one else can do it?" "Well, how are we going to finish the play without the actors?" At length the DIRECTOR returns to the stage.)

DIRECTOR: Uh, hello again, ladies and gentlemen. For those of you who may have forgotten, my name is *[name]*. It seems I was bit optimistic before and due to what can only be called a lessening in the number of actors usually used to finish the play, uh, we're not going to be able to continue tonight.

(From the dressing room come groans of protest.)

DIRECTOR: Well. I guess everyone's a little tense, um, anyway....

(A member of the audience throws out a question)

A: Well, why not? I mean, what happened?

DIRECTOR: What happened? Well, uh...those two women who were sitting there, um...this play is actually based in part on a true story, and those women are the real-life versions of Delia and Michelle, and, well, I guess they didn't like what they saw; sometimes I guess...

(From the dressing room the young woman who plays LYDIA calls out, "You know, this is a stupid role for me. I'm not Italian, and I'm not seventy-five.")

DIRECTOR: Yes, well, that's very helpful. Anyway...

(Another audience member calls out:)

B: Is *(Insert name of actor playing DELIA)* O K? I saw her get hit.

DIRECTOR: Yes. She's fine. She's just shaken up more than anything, but...

(Another audience member:)

C: Well, if you're not going to finish, is there some sort of refund on tickets?

DIRECTOR: A refund? Um, well, I guess...

(And another:)

D: What? You've got to be kidding me.

C: Excuse me, I wasn't talking to you.

D: You really want a refund?

DIRECTOR: Look...

C: If they're not going to finish, then yeah.

D: Well, why don't you come back and see it again?

(*Another audience member:*)

E: Look, I can't come back, so could you at least explain how it ends?

DIRECTOR: How it ends?

D: No. You've got to be kidding. Don't tell how it ends.

E: I want to know. I can't come back.

D: Well, don't ruin it for the rest of us.

DIRECTOR: Look, look. Basically it ends just like this. I hope you enjoyed it. Thank you so much for coming.

END OF PLAY

AUTHOR'S NOTES

Regarding the video: The video is a major element of the play. Although in practical terms it serves to show the fight at the end, in conceptual terms it helps to illuminate the idea of the blurred reality between person, performer, and character. The audience should never be sure which of the three they are looking at. The play is so confusing and has such a soap opera sense of who-slept-with-whom? that the video can also help the audience follow the story and keep the characters straight. There is also ample room for humor, if the video is used in the right way at the right time.

Regarding the ending: On paper the ending probably reads as a silly practical joke that will never work. In reality, however, it is quite effective. It is very powerful to watch the characters go through an hour and a half of trying to figure out what is true, and then going through it yourself for ten minutes. The director and cast should feel free to improvise and change the ending to fit their particular circumstances. Some audience members will know it's a hoax from the start. Others will always believe it was real. Most will fall in between. What is important in production is to walk that line between fiction and reality so that the truth remains its ever-elusive self.

Regarding the note at the beginning: Most of it is not true.